The Path to October 7th
Zionism's triumph, Palestine's tragedy

Karl Sabbagh

SKYSCRAPER

SKYSCRAPER PUBLICATIONS

Table of Contents

Prologue

This book deals with a topic which has, perhaps, been neglected in recent years because there has been so much else to write about, as Israel moves inexorably away from any idea of peace with the Palestinians and – under the guise of 'self-defence' – submerges itself deeper and deeper in the mire of institutionalised ethnic cleansing and anti-Palestinian racism.

The destruction and death wrought by Israel in Gaza in 2023-4 generated media headlines in the West, and affected people who had previously thought little about the Israel-Palestine dispute. Many became aware of an aspect of the Israel government's behaviour that had often been concealed from the mainstream media, or dismissed as Arab propaganda. The criminality of Israel's response to the Hamas attacks of October 7th, and the disproportionality of its onslaught, has made many – particularly younger – people realise that a conflict they may have seen as merely another international issue, with politics at its root, may not be what it seems. It is becoming clear that the Gaza war, and its extension to the Occupied West Bank, is actually the latest stage in a vengeful and vindictive war by the Jewish state against a whole people – the Palestinians – who have dared to keep alive facts about an injustice inflicted on them by Zionist Jews during the first half of the 20th century.

The injustice which led to the Arab state of Palestine being transformed into an ethnically-defined Jewish state did not stop with the declaration of the state of Israel in 1948 but has continued for the following 77 years, when the Jews have punished the Palestinians for continuing to draw attention to the theft of their land, because they did not meekly accept their status as second-class citizens of Israel itself, or as refugees scattered all over the world.

One of the early advocates of Zionism wrote: "There is no particular reason for the Arabs to cling to these few kilometres. 'To fold their tents and silently steal away' is their proverbial habit: let them exemplify it now."[1] This shows how little he – and many modern supporters of Israel – understood the natural attachment of human beings to the lands and society they have lived in for generations, an attachment which did not exist, indeed could not have existed, for the vast majority of Jews who claimed Palestine as a Jewish state.

In this book I will set out the steps that took place from 1917 onwards to deprive the Palestinian Arabs of the country they and their ancestors have lived in for centuries. They show how Zionist Jews organised a vicious, racist and mendacious project – with the help of successive British governments and, later, with the support of the United States – to promote the idea of a state in Palestine for all the Jews in the world, when many non-Zionist Jews had no interest in such an idea, and indeed have shown this by the fact that there are more Jews outside Israel than in it.

Although this book deals mainly with events in the decades leading up to 1948, it is very relevant to what is going on today, for one specific reason:

It is clear that the killings and hostage-takings of Hamas on October 7th, 2023, had causes. They were not just random occurrences like earthquakes or volcanic eruptions. But ordinary people who have tried to understand the causes have assumed that the attacks arose from some kind of grievance by Hamas against Israel's recent attacks on Palestinians in Gaza and the West Bank. People have also focussed on Hamas itself, as if the hostility to Israel was peculiar to the Islamic Resistance Movement – the meaning of its name – rather than being shared by all Palestinians.

Whether or not individual Palestinians abhor the actions taken by the militants in Hamas, the Hamas political movement continues to have the support of many Palestinians. You only have to look back to the Palestinian election of 2006, organised by the Palestine Central Election Commission, which President Jimmy Carter who was an observer described as "one of the most honest and effective [elections] I have ever known." When Hamas won a resounding victory, Carter was astonished to learn that the result would not be allowed to stand, by Israel, the US and

2

Europe, and thus the Palestinians' wishes, expressed in one of the fairest elections in the Middle East, were dismissed.

Hamas' ideology is rooted in the universal belief among Palestinians that for most of the 20th century and the first twenty-four years of the 21st the world has ignored – or been lied to about – the injustices the Palestinians have suffered. The fact that, as a result of Israel's current atrocities, that belief is now being shared by previously unaware people in the West is a small but significant source of encouragement to Palestinians.

But there is still a lot of work to do before the truth about Israel and Palestine is understood outside the parties involved. Israel and its supporters have no shame when it comes to presenting myths about the origins of the dispute, and in this book I will try to bring a few facts to bear on the tissue of lies that are purveyed in numerous websites, articles and books, and by Israel's representatives abroad, who are truly examples of that definition of an ambassador by Sir Henry Wotton, as someone 'sent to lie abroad for his country'.*

In setting out how the malign actions of Zionist Jews between 1917 and 1948 created the catastrophe suffered by all Palestinians, I have no illusions that, overnight, a wave of comprehension will sweep over the world and lead to some kind of rectification of all the wrongs done to Palestinians. Israel and its allies are far more powerful than a single book can ever be, in their access to mass media, members of parliament or Congress, and sources of huge funding for their propaganda. They also have a shield to minimise any attempt to tell the truth about the actions of the Zionist movement and Israel over the last 120 years – the accusation that any criticisms of Israel are motivated by antisemitism.

I hope anyone reading this book will take such accusations with a pinch of salt. The hysteria generated by Israel and its supporters over the widespread demonstrations of support for Palestinians during their recent sufferings should be

---

*Often misquoted as 'sent abroad to lie for his country'. The correct version is a play on words. 'To lie abroad' used to mean to stay somewhere away from home.

treated with the contempt it deserves. Like that mythical creature the 'self-hating Jew', the 'antisemitic supporter of Palestine' is a far rarer creature than Israel makes out. Many demonstrators against Israel's actions in Gaza are Jews themselves, and since many 'real' antisemites are racists, it is unlikely that they spend much time agonising over the injustices done to two million Palestinians, who are also, of course, Semites.

In the House of Commons in January 1948, the British Foreign Secretary, Ernest Bevin, said the following:

> "The Arabs feel as profoundly as the Jews that in the problem of Palestine right is on their side. They consider that for the Arab population, which has been occupying Palestine for more than 20 centuries, to be turned out of their lands and homes to make way for another race is a profound injustice. We understand how this strikes the Arabs – all the Arab people, not only their Governments – and we should consider how the British people would have reacted if a similar demand had been made on us. Suppose we had been asked to give up a slice of Scotland, Wales or Cornwall to another race, and that the present inhabitants had been compelled to make way. I think there might have been trouble in this House, and possibly outside."[2]

It might be added that if, in addition, the Scots, Welsh or Cornish had been persistently accused of fabricating the history of their dispossession, their sense of grievance and desire for redress might have been all the greater.

I should make clear one thing about the terminology I use to name the opponents of the Palestinians. From time to time, I use the word 'Jews' or 'Jewish' to describe people or organisations. I do this for several reasons. First, there were no Israelis before 1948, when the Palestinians were being attacked by people who were undoubtedly Jews. Second, the people who claimed Palestine called themselves 'Jews' even though there were plenty of Jews who did not share their racist beliefs about the Palestinians. Third, those who supported the acquisition of Palestine defined their aim as 'a Jewish state' and today Israel hammers home the idea that it is 'the Jewish state'. We call the actions of the French state French actions, so why shouldn't we call the actions of the Jewish state 'Jewish actions' and condemn them in those terms when necessary? (In fact, of course, Palestinian Arabs live in Israel as well, even today, making up 20% of the population.)

I also use the word 'Zionists' to distinguish Jews who believe that it was – and is – permissible to occupy the Arab state of Palestine from the sizeable number who don't.

Arthur Balfour, Herbert Samuel and Chaim Weizmann,
three Zionists who transformed Palestine.

Chapter 1: The Big Lie

In 2023 I wrote to the BBC about what I saw as an error on their website. In an account of the Arab-Israel dispute, the website said:

> "The Jewish leadership in Palestine declared the establishment of the State of Israel on 14 May 1948, the moment the British mandate terminated, though without announcing its borders. The following day Israel was invaded by five Arab armies, marking the start of Israel's War of Independence."[3]

Setting aside the logical conundrum that it is difficult to see how a state which hadn't (and still hasn't) defined its borders can claim to have been invaded, this is a factually incorrect statement of what Arab armies did on May 14th. It is factually incorrect for a purpose. Israel and its supporters want people to believe that when Israelis fought a war against Arabs in 1948, it was because their new state was being invaded.

The BBC were not alone in printing this statement. In fact, whoever wrote the text for the BBC website was probably comforted by the fact that a brief internet search would have shown that his or her belief was shared by dozens if not hundreds of other sources.

Here's a selection of other statements about the same issue which, as I will show in this book, are factually incorrect:

> "… the Arab armies invaded Israel on the very day of its birth, May 15, 1948…"[4]

> "Six months later, on May 14, 1948, Jewish leaders in the region formed the state of Israel. British troops left, thousands of Palestinian Arabs fled and Arab armies invaded Israel."[5]

> "The Arab armies invaded Israel after its declaration of independence, on May 15th…"[6]

> "The Arab armies invaded Israel from all sides, and fierce fighting ensued as the poorly-equipped Israel Defense Forces struggled to fight back…"[7]

"Rabin ... recalled that in 1947-48, when the Arab armies invaded Israel ..."[8]

"On May 15, 1948, the first day of Israeli Independence and exactly one year after UNSCOP was established, Arab armies invaded Israel and the Arab-Israeli War of 1948 began."[9]

"Five Arab armies and contingents from two more, equipped with modern tanks, artillery, and warplanes invaded Israel from north, east, and south. Total war was forced on the *Yishuv* under the most difficult conditions."[10]

"In 1948, when six Arab armies invaded the Jewish state in order to destroy it on the very day of its birth..."[11]

"Immediately after the declaration an all-out war broke out between the Jews and Arabs, seven Arab armies attacked the new Jewish State..."[12]

To understand why the statements listed above are wrong, I need to address the following question:

WHAT DID THE WORD 'ISRAEL' MEAN ON MAY 15TH, 1948?

In the Eastern Mediterranean, between the Jordan river and the Mediterranean Sea, there existed a single country called Palestine between 1918 and 1948. In this country were cities, towns and villages, inhabited largely by Palestinian Arabs, both Muslim and Christian, along with much smaller numbers of Jews. Before the First World War, Palestine was part of the Ottoman, or Turkish, Empire, along with other Arab territories such as Syria, Iraq and parts of Arabia. After the War, from 1918, Palestine fell under the control of the British. For the ordinary Palestinians, the machinations of the Great Powers went on above their heads as they went about their daily lives. Their identities did not change as one ruler was replaced by another. They were Palestinian Arabs and had been for generations, and the country they lived in was Palestine. The only 'Israel' they had heard of was somewhere inhabited over 2000 years ago by adherents of Judaism and described in their Bible as occupying an area which varied from a small part of today's West Bank to, at times, covering most of the Middle East as far east as the Arabian Gulf.

So what, or where, was the 'Israel' that was allegedly attacked by Arab armies on May 15th, 1948?

A clue is in the phrase 'the Jewish state' used in a couple of the quotes at the top of the chapter. For reasons I shall explore later, the United Nations General Assembly had voted in November 1947 to set specific areas of Palestine aside for a Jewish state and others for the Palestinian Arabs.

During decades of attempts to take over some or all of Palestine, a political group of Jews called Zionists* decided that if they could persuade Britain or other world powers to create a Jewish state in Palestine they would call it 'Israel', and so when the British left Palestine on May 14th, 1948, the Zionist movement declared that the area allocated to them by the UN was now a state called Israel.

The significance of this is that *when Arab armies entered the much larger area of Palestine on May 15th they did not attack the Jewish area allocated in the Partition plan,* which is the only interpretation we can make of the word 'Israel' at that point. Although it turned out that the Jews were not particularly happy with the area allocated to them, *it was the only 'Israel' the UN had voted for,* and the only Israel that existed on May 15th, when, for reasons I will also explain below, Arab armies moved into *Palestine.*

Of course, if the representatives of the Jews were allowed to define the *whole* of Palestine, including the Arab areas, as 'Israel', then we would have to admit that Arab armies had actually entered 'Israel'. But much as the Jews of Palestine would like to have laid claim to the whole of Palestine – and they had certainly tried in the past – the Zionist movement had said, at least publicly, that they accepted the smaller area in the UN Partition plan.

It is interesting that in later pro-Israel accounts of the events, on those occasions where, perhaps, some vague degree of factual accuracy is felt to be desirable, reports talk of Arab

---

* 'Zion' is a Hebrew name for Jerusalem

8

armies invading 'Palestine' not Israel. By a kind of sleight of hand, a reader who is not concentrating is encouraged to find it reprehensible that Arab armies are actually entering an area allocated to the Palestinian Arabs, in order to protect them.

In fact, Palestinians in the areas allocated to the Arab state were only too pleased to see *any* Arab armies, to augment the measly resources they had themselves. As I will show later, this was not just because a new and possibly hostile state was about to be formed on their borders but because the Palestinian Arabs had already experienced Jewish attacks on Palestinians long before May 15th 1948 *in the areas allocated to the Palestinian Arabs in the UN plan.*

The phrase 'Arab armies', or in the case of the BBC, 'five Arab armies' or of the FLAME website 'six Arab armies', or the Jewish history website 'seven Arab armies', refers to the help given to the Palestinians by the forces of the neighbouring Arab countries, although one of the five, six, or seven armies, the Lebanese, didn't even enter Palestine, let alone 'Israel'.

There were five Arab countries surrounding the British-controlled territory of Palestine, which had armies which sought to enter Palestine (not Israel) on May 15th. Palestine and its majority Arab population were important to these countries. There was a shared language, Arabic, and a majority shared religion, Islam. In addition, there were Holy Places in Jerusalem, to which Muslim pilgrims came from other countries.

Those five countries were Lebanon, to the north, Syria to the north-east, Iraq to the east, Jordan to the southeast, and Egypt to the southwest. Never mentioned in the quotes above, is the contribution of the Palestinian Arabs themselves, who lived throughout Palestine, both in the area allocated to the Jews in the Partition plan, and the area allocated for their own state. Clearly, they too had reasons, stronger reasons even than an alliance with a neighbouring country, to object to the takeover of a large section of their former country by a Jewish state. Thousands of poorly armed Palestinians were prepared to defend their homes and families and there were 5-6,000 Arab irregulars from neighbouring countries.

But if, as I say, the armies did not enter the Jewish area of partitioned Palestine – Israel – why were they in Palestine at all? You get the impression from Israeli accounts of the events of 1947-48, that all Israel wanted was to be allowed to set up the Jewish state in Palestine within borders ordained by the UN General Assembly, and to live in peace and harmony with the neighbouring Palestinian state in the rest of Palestine.

In 1949, after 750,000 Palestinians had been expelled from their homes (or left voluntarily, as apologists for Israel still say), a British Jewish M.P., Sidney Silverman, said in the House of Commons, in reply to a speech by the Foreign Secretary, Ernest Bevin:

> "I am sure my right hon. Friend knows perfectly well that, so far from driving anybody away, [the Israel government] did their utmost to persuade them to stay, [and] that those who did stay were very well treated..."[13]

A character called Captain Renault in the film *Casablanca*, when accused of running a gambling den, says "I'm shocked, shocked to find that gambling is going on in here!" when he was, of course, a participant. It reminds me of how supporters of Israel pretend to be shocked that thousands of Palestinians left their homes when Israel was declared, instead of rushing into the open arms of a benign and welcoming Jewish community.

But in fact, by May 14th, 1948, *every* Palestinian had many reasons to fear for the future of herself, her family, her home and her community. When the Arab armies moved into Palestine on May 15th they were trying to prevent the aims of a concerted anti-Palestinian campaign by Zionism – which had lasted for thirty years – to deprive the Palestinian Arabs of their rights and, if possible, their lives, and take over their land.

In 2007, a book was published called *If I Did It*. It had been written by O.J. Simpson, the disgraced ex-football player and actor who had been acquitted in 1994 of murdering his wife and her friend, and the thesis of the book was 'I didn't murder my wife and her friend, but if I had, this is how and why I would have done it.' I am going to take a similar approach. Arab armies *didn't* invade Israel on May 15th, but I shall explain why they had very good reasons to do so and that by stopping at the border of the Jewish state they were exercising remarkable restraint in the face of huge provocation.

The focus of this book is the growing realisation among Palestinians after the First World War that their very existence in their homeland, of which they had formed the indigenous population for centuries, was under threat from a European political movement, Zionism.

This realisation came about slowly because Palestinians, who believed they had as firm an entitlement to live in an independent state of their own as any other nation, could not believe that that entitlement would be ignored by a conglomerate of Western states which had just won a war to bring democracy and freedom to colonised peoples. But slowly, a number of factors in the treatment of Palestine in the years leading up to 1948 showed the Palestinians that their whole way of life was under threat and that, while colonialism might have been eradicated in the rest of the world, it was alive and well in the treatment of the Palestinian people.

Those factors were:

- Anti-Palestinian racism
- Immigration of foreigners to Palestine
- Preferential treatment of the growing Jewish community in Palestine
- The injustice of partition i.e. taking away part of Palestine from Arabs
- The rigged vote for partition at the UN.
- Increasing Jewish violence against Palestinians

One by one, these factors – ignored by the rest of the world – combined to form a cumulative denial of the rights of the Palestinian people during the 1920s, '30s and '40s, a denial they saw could lead inexorably to the loss of their land to a group of people, Zionist Jews, who had no legal right to take it over.

In the rest of this book, I will explore this accumulation of anti-Palestinian factors one by one and suggest that they eventually forced ordinary Palestinians to realise – too late – that they were the victims of a major injustice, an injustice which is still imposed on Palestinians today by Israel and its Western supporters.

This exploration will also help clarify what really happened in 1948 and show that it was Israel that invaded Palestine, rather than the Arab armies invading Israel, and that the war in Gaza was merely a continuation of Israel's century-long antagonism to Palestinians for not abandoning their claim to their ancestral home.

Chapter 2: The 'non-Jews' of Palestine

Perhaps the first and most enduring factor in the whole sad story of the loss of Palestine is the contempt shown towards Palestinians, and indeed towards all Arabs, by Zionists from the very beginning of their attempts to take over Palestine.

It is possible – just – to imagine a situation in which a group of well-meaning Jews approached the British seeking help in building a post-War state of Palestine in partnership with the indigenous Arab population, where Jews could come and live and share in the development of the country.

The sort of person who wrote the following, for example, would surely not devote his life to the theft of a whole country and the oppression of its indigenous inhabitants:

> "The Jewish nation has stood from time immemorial for the loftiest of spiritual ideals; its life through two thousand years of exile has been one long tribute to the supremacy of the things of the spirit; the record of the Zionist movement itself is proof of the power of an ideal to stir the Jewish people to-day to new life and heroic effort."[14]

But in fact, such lofty ideals were spelled out by a Zionist, Chaim Weizmann, whose 'heroic effort' was dedicated over three decades to imposing a huge injustice on Palestine and the Palestinians.

Of course, any genuine approach to a Jewish participation in post-War Palestine would involve words like 'partnership' and 'sharing' and require Jews to accept that Arabs had similar political rights, something which as it turned out, no Zionist Jew was ever willing to contemplate.

It's a shame that there is no equivalent word to 'antisemitism' to apply to expressions of hatred or prejudice against Arabs. The drip drip drip of anti-Arab sentiments, from senior figures and even official bodies during decades of discussions of the claims of the indigenous population of Palestine to independence showed the contempt that Zionists and their British supporters had for the people whose land they coveted. Private correspondence and confidential government papers are replete with anti-Arab racism at the same time that Jews were expressing a desire for a shared coexistence in Palestine in the public statements of the framers and supporters of the Jewish 'National Home' as it was called.

It's worth considering what cries of 'antisemitism' there would be if the following quotes, were about Jewish communities rather than the Arab ones they describe:

> "We must not forget that we are dealing here with a semi-savage people, which has extremely primitive concepts. And this is his nature: If he senses in you power, he will submit and will hide his hatred for you. And if he senses weakness, he will dominate you ... Moreover ... owing to the many tourists and urban Christians, there developed among the Arabs base values which are not common among other primitive people ... to lie, to cheat, to harbor grave [unfounded] suspicions and to tell tales.... and a hidden hatred for the Jews. These Semites – they are anti-Semites." [15]

> "In 1920, Israel Zangwill said: 'If the Lord Shaftesbury was literally inexact in describing Palestine as a country without a people, he was essentially correct, for there is no Arab people living in intimate fusion with the country, utilizing its resources and stamping it with a characteristic impress: there is at best an Arab encampment.'"[16]

> "Perhaps this war [WW1] has revealed most clearly the need which the Near East has of modern, progressive development. A vast stretch of territory bordering on the Mediterranean, on the Indian Ocean, and on the Euphrates, sparsely populated by a semi-backward people with a low standard of living, presented, so to say, a vacuum and a prey to any predatory country, and this made the Arab population peculiarly receptive to Nazi-Fascist propaganda."[17]

> CHAIM WEIZMANN: "[the indigenous population [of Palestine is akin to] the rocks of Judea, as obstacles that have to be cleared on a difficult path."[18]

> ZE'EV JABOTINSKY: "We Jews, thank God, have nothing to do with the East. ... The Islamic soul must be broomed [sic] out of Eretz-

Yisrael ... [Muslims are] yelling rabble dressed up in gaudy, savage rags."[19]

AHAD HA'AM: "We are used to thinking of the Arabs as primitive men of the desert, as a donkey-like nation that neither sees nor understands what is going around it. But this is a great error. The Arab, like all sons of Sham, has sharp and crafty mind ... Should time come when life of our people in Palestine imposes to a smaller or greater extent on the natives, they will not easily step aside."[20]

This contempt for the Palestinians had existed in the West from the time the Zionist Jews of Europe first cast envious eyes on Palestine. Part of that contempt is shown in the way in which the population of Palestine has been denigrated as 'peasants' or 'bedouin' and the land of Palestine as arid, deserted, and crying out for the talents of Jews to fertilise it. Two examples show this deception at work.

In 1869, Mark Twain published a book called *The Innocents Abroad*, telling the story of a group of American tourists to the Holy Land. One particular quotation from that book has achieved viral fame by being included in dozens if not hundreds of pro-Israel websites, articles, and books. It clearly resonates with Israel's supporters because, in their view, it proves that Palestine was empty in the 19th century.

The quote is:

"Stirring scenes ... occur in the valley [Jezreel] no more. There is not a solitary village throughout its whole extent – not for thirty miles in either direction. There are two or three small clusters of Bedouin tents, but not a single permanent habitation. One may ride ten miles hereabouts and not see ten human beings."[21]

Quite how one paragraph by one observer about one small area of Palestine can carry such a weight of proof as to justify the argument that Palestine should be taken over by Jews is never made clear, let alone a paragraph written by one of America's leading humourists who, elsewhere in the book, claims – equally believably – "We were compelled to jump over upwards of eighteen hundred donkeys."

In any case, the quote is a lie. A short visit to Israel, the West Bank and Gaza will reveal hundreds of Arab towns and villages with histories of continuous population that stretch back at least to the eighteenth century and many for hundreds of years before that. And there are many reliable sources that back this up.

The market place in Tiberias, one of many ancient Palestinian towns with varied and thriving populations at a time when the Zionists described Palestinians as "yelling rabble."

For example, here are more quotes describing Palestine at the same period:

"Here were evidences of cultivation, an acre or two of rich soil studded with last season's dead corn-stalks of the thickness of your thumb and very wide apart. ... it was a thrilling spectacle. ... The view presented from its highest peak was almost beautiful. Below, was the broad, level plain of Esdraelon, [also known as the Vale of Jezreel] checkered with fields like a chess-board, and full as smooth and level, seemingly; dotted about its borders with white, compact villages, and faintly penciled, far and near, with the curving lines of roads and trails. When it is robed in the fresh verdure of spring, it must form a charming picture, even by itself. Nazareth is wonderfully interesting... We found here a grove of lemon trees -- cool, shady, hung with fruit ..."[22] etc, etc, etc.

16

Now why didn't these websites, books and articles quote *this* evidence, that Palestine was populated and fertile in the 19th century, particularly since it was by the same author, Mark Twain, from the same book, *The Innocents Abroad*, on whose account they placed such reliance? The question hardly needs to be asked.

One more example out of many helps to show the continuity of deception practiced by Zionists and their supporters over a hundred years, in order to deny the history, culture and political rights of the Palestinians. This comes from a book called *Promised Land*, published in 1947, eighty years after Mark Twain's 'not a single human habitation'.

> "Palestine is a very small country, and more than two-thirds of it have been laid waste during the almost two thousand years of foreign rule. Where in Biblical times millions of people lived on fertile soil, only a few thousand Bedouins could graze their meagre cattle only a few decades ago, when a handful of Jewish peasants started their giant struggle for soil reclamation."[23]

'A few decades' before this book was published, the population of Palestine was over 600,000, mainly Arab and very few of them Bedouins, and the farmers and merchants who exported the famous Jaffa oranges to Europe would have been surprised to learn that they were living and farming in a land which had largely been laid waste.

Unfortunately, some people were (and are) naïve enough to believe this sort of tosh, and they were easy prey for the group of European Zionists who set themselves the task of persuading the British government to support their aim of turning Arab Palestine into a Jewish state.

In 1917, Britain issued the so-called 'Balfour Declaration' stating that after the Great War was won and Palestine was free of Ottoman control, the country should become the location of a Jewish 'National Home'.

The wording was as follows:

> "His Majesty's Government view with favour the establishment in Palestine of a National Home for the Jewish people, and will use their best endeavours to facilitate the achievement of this

object, it being clearly understood that nothing shall be done which may prejudice the civil and religious rights of existing non-Jewish communities in Palestine, or the rights and political status enjoyed by Jews in any other country."

The declaration used the phrase 'National Home', so as not to alarm the Palestinian Arabs – 90% of the population – because it allowed the Zionists to deny publicly at that time that they wanted to turn the whole of Palestine into a Jewish state. In fact, the Declaration itself barely recognised that there *were* Arabs in Palestine. The only reference in the Declaration to the majority Palestinian community was "existing *non-Jewish* communities in Palestine…" It is as if a British government statement about immigration in 2025 said something like "our current plans for immigration into the UK will not affect the rights of the *non-immigrant* population," i.e. the British.

There are plenty of detailed accounts of the history of the Balfour Declaration, but I'd like to analyse just one aspect: the fact that it was not drawn up by the British government at all but was actually written by a group of Zionists and handed to Arthur Balfour, then the Foreign Secretary, to sign. It has been presented to the world as a statement of British foreign policy as Britain emerged from the First World War and considered the new situation after the defeat of Germany and their Turkish allies. But in fact the people who wrote it had no interest in doing what was good for Britain, but merely what was good for Jews, or for one specific group of Jews, Zionists, since there were other Jews in Britain and Europe who disagreed with the whole idea of turning Palestine into a Jewish state.

The group who wrote the Balfour Declaration was led by Harry Sacher, a 36-year-old journalist. At the time he was on the staff of the *Manchester Guardian*, and a passionate Zionist. He was also very close to Chaim Weizmann, who wrote to him as "Darling Harry" and signed his letters "Love, Chaim."[24]

Sacher wrote to Weizmann: "It is good news that B[alfour] wants us to frame a declaration and I shall be happy to try my hand at a draft."

The thought of this young journalist 'trying his hand at a draft' of a declaration of British government policy on the Middle East, at the request of the British Foreign Minister, is an indication of how complete the victory was by this early stage in the Zionist onslaught on Whitehall.

The group of political Zionists got out their pens or sat at their typewriters, and began to turn out draft declarations of what they wanted the British to do about Palestine.

Sacher's first thoughts, set out in a letter to Weizmann in June 1917, were Machiavellian: "I should like it to be at once precise and vague, precise in what it excludes, vague in the means by which what we want is to be realised."[25]

Within a month Sacher and other members of the group had produced several different drafts which were gathered together and sent to Leon Simon, a sympathetic Jewish member of the Civil Service, for him to combine the best ideas in one version.

There were six drafts of varying lengths, all promising that Palestine would be recognised as the National Home of the Jewish people and a Jewish state, "Jewish in the same sense as the dominant national character of England is English, of Canada Canadian and of Australia Australian." This last phrase occurred in the draft written by another Guardian journalist, Herbert Sidebotham.

None of these drafts made any reference at all to the existing population of Palestine, 90% of them Palestinian Arabs. But occasionally, in the Zionist files dealing with that period, there are references to the Arab inhabitants. In a letter from Harry Sacher to Leon Simon, Sacher wrote:

> "At the back of my mind there is firmly fixed the recognition that even if all our political schemings turn out in the way we desire, the Arabs will remain our most tremendous problem."[26]

He got that right.

Sacher's draft of what was to become the Balfour Declaration was very different from the final version, but it reveals that what the Zionists really wanted was total control of Palestine, with no political participation by the indigenous population in their own government.

Adopting a cloak of authority somewhat grander than his job as a *Guardian* journalist, Sacher began his draft with the words:

> "The British Government declares..." and went on to describe an essential war aim as "the reconstitution of Palestine as a Jewish state and as the National Home of the Jewish people."[27]

Every word in every draft was carefully chosen. There is a revealing analysis of the importance of one two-letter word in Sacher's draft which shows this starkly.

> "I beg you to note the phrase 'the reconstitution of Palestine'; '*of*' not '*in*'," Sacher wrote to another member of the group. "The 'of' is fundamental. It is our charter against Arab domination ... We must control the <u>state</u> machinery in Palestine: if we don't the Arabs will. Give the Arabs all the guarantees they like for cultural autonomy; but the state must be Jewish."[28]

In spite of all the evidence to the contrary, even today there are people who believe that Arthur Balfour wrote the letter above his signature. One recent writer says:

> "Ever since, people have been struggling to understand just what exactly that statement means; a sign of [Balfour's] masterful usage of the English language to mean different things to different people."[29]

The masterful ambiguity was Zionism's contribution, not Balfour's.

The 'Balfour' Declaration was sent as a letter to a leading British Jew, Walter Rothschild, in November 1917, and then the British government and its allies got on with winning the War. As it stood, it was just a statement that the British government 'viewed with favour' the aims of the Zionists. Viewing something with favour is certainly not committing to do something. I view with favour eating healthily but that doesn't mean I am legally obliged to do so. Nevertheless, ever since, the letter has been treated by supporters of Zionism as if it was a binding legal obligation on the British government.

The letter could have remained locked away in Lord Rothschild's filing cabinet for evermore, had it not been for the fact that it was designed as the first step in a Zionist campaign to turn it into some kind of binding legal document.

Everyone knew that when the War was over and Turkey, Germany's ally, was defeated, the countries of the former Ottoman empire would wish to move towards independence. One of these countries was Palestine, and the Palestinians were entitled to the same rights as other subjugated peoples who expected to be given their independence after the War. In particular, as the victorious nations assembled in Paris for the Peace Conference, the Palestinians were entitled to expect that they would benefit from one of US President Wilson's Fourteen Aims, spelled out as the War drew to a close, which included:

> "The ... nationalities which are now under Turkish rule should be assured an ... absolutely unmolested opportunity of autonomous development."[30]

In the view of the Great Powers, this 'unmolested autonomous development' should be supervised by the newly formed League of Nations which would allocate a 'Mandate' for each of the countries in question to one of the victorious allies. The Mandates would consist of sets of instructions for each territory, and the supervising nation, the 'Mandatory', would then manage the post-war administration of the specific country, helping it to build up its own administrative structures until it could take over from the Mandate holder and govern itself.

These matters were settled at peace talks in Paris, where the victorious nations gathered to make decisions about the reshaping of the post-war world, and position papers were compiled by civil servants to be circulated among the delegates. The British section on Palestine in a 12-page document on the 'Settlement of the Middle East' has Zionist fingerprints all over it. Here's part of what it says:

"His Majesty's Government consider that [the problems of Palestine] can be dealt with by the Conference through a mandate conferred upon a single Power.*... the principle terms of reference being as follows: (a) to set up the framework of a Palestinian state, of which all inhabitants of the country would be citizens, with equal civil rights, irrespective of nationality or creed; (b) to secure for the two main elements in the population, the Zionist Jews and the Arabs, representation on the Palestinian administration in proportion to their respective stakes in the country: c) to train the two elements to work together, so that they should be able, at the earliest possible moment, to govern themselves..."[31]

A couple of questions arise here. For example, why would His Majesty's government specify Jews as one of the two main elements in the Palestinian population? At the time, the number of all Jews in Palestine was less 10%, hardly a 'main element.' And why '*Zionist* Jews'? What about non-Zionist Jews? Or secular Jews? There were certainly some of these in Palestine in 1919. But since these documents were written by, or under the influence of, the Zionist movement, and the whole project to turn Palestine into a Jewish state was the pet project of Zionists, the needs of non-Zionist Jews might be deemed to be irrelevant.

Also, what does "representation on the Palestinian administration in proportion to their respective stakes in the country" mean? Why not the principle of representation adopted all over the world, i.e. in proportion *to their numbers in the population*? Of course, the answer is obvious. By dropping in a vague word like 'stake', the definition of exactly which Palestinians would have how much say in the government of the new nation could be left till later.

Patronising as the Mandates scheme sounds, this arrangement could have worked out well for Iraq, Syria and Palestine. Each country had its own unique historical and

---

* Guess which 'single Power' is intended.

social factors, which might have led to slightly different Mandates, but they could all have become independent within a few years. In fact, under this system Iraq gained its independence in 1932 and Syria in 1946.

But the last thing the Zionists wanted was for the population of Palestine as it was in 1921 to become independent, since this would stop the country ever becoming a Jewish state. The first step in thwarting 'autonomous development' for Palestine was to ensure that Great Britain, already favourably inclined towards Zionism, was granted the Mandate for Palestine. The second was to transform the message in the 'viewing with favour' letter, the Balfour Declaration, into a binding commitment to turn Palestine into a Jewish state. They did this with the help of their friends in the British government, by incorporating the wording of the Balfour Declaration in the text of the League of Nations Mandate. The relevant section, Article 2, said:

> "The Mandatory shall be responsible for placing the country under such political, administrative and economic conditions as will secure the establishment of the Jewish national home, as laid down in the preamble [quoted from the Balfour Declaration], and the development of self-governing institutions, and also for safeguarding the civil and religious rights of all the inhabitants of Palestine, irrespective of race and religion."[32]

If there were any Palestinians who had not become cynical about the growing relationship between the Zionists and the British government, they might have taken heart when they read in the Mandate about Britain being required to secure 'the development of self-governing institutions', and indeed, there were times in the next twenty years where Britain assured the Palestinian Arabs that they were really going to try very hard to do just that. After all, the word 'and' implied that *both* a Jewish National Home *and* the development of self-governing institutions were required and possible under the terms of the Mandate. Certainly, if the 'Jewish National

Home' phrase meant something less than a complete takeover of Palestine, this might be achievable.

In a later chapter, we will see how the Zionists treated the '*and*' in Article 2 as an '*or*' as soon as any attempts were made by British civil servants or unbiassed ministers to devise a Legislative Council for Palestine. For the Zionists, self-governing institutions for the population of Palestine would negate their aim of taking over the country and making it 'as Jewish as England is English', as Weizmann notoriously put it, and would have to be resisted by every measure, at least as long as the Palestinian Arabs were in a majority.

Chapter 3: The new democracy

The hostility of Zionist Jews to the Arabs as expressed in the Balfour Declaration and elsewhere seemed to have two main causes. First, the Palestinian Arabs were the predominant population in a territory the Jews wanted for themselves. This was not, of course, the Arabs' fault, but you could see how it might not endear them to the Jews. But the second was more directly 'the Arabs' fault', in one sense.

In all the discussion of the Jewish National Home, the point was made frequently that the Arabs were an inferior people who could not be trusted to govern themselves and were certainly not as talented or as wealthy as the Jews. (Sacher once made a remark to the effect that "he would not believe an Arab under oath"[33]) Of course, this was irrelevant both to the nature of the right of self-determination the Palestinians might claim and, indeed, to whether this 'inferiority' automatically granted the Jews of the world the right to take over the Palestinians' land. Nevertheless, it was a point often made by the Zionists in Europe and America as if it *was* relevant.

Sacher wrote an article called *A Jewish Palestine* in July 1919 in the *Atlantic* magazine. He made only two references to the Arab population at the time: "The Jewish Palestine will strive [for] a harmonious cooperation between Jew, Arab, and Armenian." (Sacher's grasp of Palestinian demography was pretty shaky. The Armenians formed a quarter of a percent of the population at the time.) The other reference, not even using the word 'Arab', was: "[The Jewish people] are … anxious that the rights of the cultivating fellaheen shall be conserved, and there is plenty of room for the fellaheen and for the Jewish immigrants."

'Fellaheen' are defined as 'peasants or agricultural labourers.' Along with many Zionists, Sacher believed, or pretended to believe, that there were no Arab teachers, doctors, lawyers, merchants, administrators, shopkeepers, builders, architects, train drivers, secretaries, accountants, barbers, mayors, restaurateurs, waiters, or capitalists in

Palestine, merely 'fellaheen', ploughing fields, planting crops, and spreading manure.

But any moves toward self-governance for Palestine – i.e. democracy – would pose a problem for a Jewish state in Palestine unless some way could be found to redefine the word 'democracy'. In the normal sense of the word, a democratic Palestine would require voting rights for all inhabitants, Arabs and Jews (and Armenians). But in a document Sacher wrote for the Zionist Organisation, he explained that what most people in the West understood as democracy was not suitable for a country like Palestine:

> "Democracy in America too commonly means majority rule, without regard to diversities of types or stages of civilization or differences of quality. ... This doubtless is natural in America, and works on the whole very well. But if the American idea were applied as an American administration might apply it to Palestine, what would happen? The numerical majority in Palestine today is Arab, not Jewish. Qualitatively [sic], it is a simple fact that the Jews are now predominant in Palestine* and given proper conditions they will be predominant quantitatively also in a generation or two. But if the crude arithmetical conception of democracy were to be applied now, or at some early stage in the future to Palestinian conditions, the majority that would rule would be the Arab majority, and the task of establishing and developing a great Jewish Palestine would be infinitely more difficult."[34]

This extraordinary statement, although written by Sacher, a man prone to extraordinary statements, was sanctioned by the whole Zionist Organisation, since it was in a publication they organised to put their case for a Jewish Palestine to the general public. Fortunately – for the rest of the world at least – the 'crude arithmetical conception' of democracy is the one that has caught on in global politics. Without it, Catholics and Protestants in Northern Ireland, Sunnis in Iraq, even perhaps university graduates in the United Kingdom would each be

---

* Quantitatively, they were 9% of the population.

trying to make a case for ruling over their qualitatively less predominant fellow-citizens.

Delusional as this idea is, it was supported by Balfour himself. In July 1920, in a speech to the Zionist Federation at the Albert Hall, Balfour said:

> "The critics of this [Zionist] movement shelter themselves behind … the principle of self-determination, and say that, if you apply that principle logically and honestly, it is to the majority of the existing population of Palestine that the future destinies of Palestine should be committed. My lords, ladies and gentlemen, there is a technical ingenuity in that plea, and on technical grounds I neither can nor desire to provide the answer; but, looking back upon the history of the world, I say that the case of Jewry in all countries is absolutely exceptional, falls outside all the ordinary rules and maxims, cannot be contained in a formula or explained in a sentence. The deep, underlying principle of self-determination really points to a Zionist policy, however little in its strict technical interpretation it may seem to favour it."[35]

Nothing illustrates better Balfour's reckless carelessness with facts and issues of justice than this quote. But then many of the people who came in touch with Balfour were unimpressed by him. Winston Churchill said "If you wanted nothing done, Arthur Balfour was the best man for the task. There was no equal to him."

Although the intention behind the Balfour Declaration was to turn Palestine into a Jewish state, this could not be admitted publicly, and so the Zionists' statements were littered with Jewish denials of any such intention:

> "Only those suffering from gross ignorance, or actuated by malice, could accuse us of the desire of establishing an independent Jewish kingdom. … The aim of Zionism is the erection for the Jewish people of a publicly recognized, legally secured home in Palestine. Not a Jewish state but a home in the ancient land of our forefathers, where we can live a Jewish life without oppression and persecution. … That and nothing else is our aim."[36]

"[In 1918] Dr Weizmann ... told [leading Palestinians] it was his ambition to see Palestine governed by some stable government like that of Great Britain, that a Jewish government would be fatal to his plans and that it was simply his wish to provide a home for the Jews in the Holy Land where they could live their own national life, sharing equal rights with the other inhabitants."[37]

Weizmann writing to *The Times*: "It is not likely that there will ever be an 'Arab question' in Palestine: non-Jews need not fear that they will suffer at our hands. For two thousand years we have known what it means to be strangers. We Jews know the heart of the stranger: are we likely to deal out oppression?"[38]

"The terms of the declaration referred to do not contemplate that Palestine as a whole should be converted into a Jewish National Home, but that such a Home should be founded 'in Palestine.'"[39]

MOSES GASTER: "It has been said, and is still being obstinately repeated by anti-Zionists again and again, that Zionism aims at the creation of an independent 'Jewish state.' But this is wholly fallacious. The 'Jewish state' was never part of the Zionist programme."[40]

LORD ROTHSCHILD TO BALFOUR: "One of the chief aims of the Zionist Federation, when the settlement in Palestine takes place, is to see that while obtaining as large a measure of autonomy as possible, no encroachment on the rights of the other inhabitants of the country should take place..."[41]

"The danger to which the Arabs are allegedly exposed as a result of Jewish work is imaginary, not real. The penetration into Semitic countries in general and into Palestine in particular of a Semitic race will result in no danger to the Arabs. On the contrary, it will contribute to its vigour and to its inherent strength. We Jews shall not thrust ourselves an alien growth upon the body politic of the Arabs, as many extreme nationalists believe, but we shall form a beautiful ring in the chain of the United Arab Confederation."[42]

"I have it on the highest authority from one intimate of Lord Balfour that a political Jewish state was not thought of in 1917. An intimate friend, (a British Jew) of Dr. Weizmann states that the latter at that time did not intend a Jewish state, but that he was drawn to political Zionism some years later."[43]

This litany of lies is only the first of many such collections of quotes in this book. The reader may feel that she had got the point after reading the first few, but one purpose of this book is to show that *nothing* said by Zionist Jews about Palestinians in public can be trusted without independent corroboration, since their public statements are composed to disadvantage Palestinians at every turn as they try to get their case heard. Former Israeli prime minister and terrorist Yitzhak Shamir later declared openly that "it is permissible to lie for the sake of the Land of Israel," something he did many times. There is no doubt that almost everyone who made the statements above knew that he was lying.

Most participants in those early discussions, British and Jewish, denied in public what they plotted in private to bring about. As we've seen with Harry Sacher's jejune ramblings, there is copious evidence among the Zionists' own archives, as well as those of Britain and the US, that from the beginning of attempts to influence the British government right through the period of the Mandate the ultimate aim was to turn the whole of Palestine into a Jewish state:

"Dr Moses Gaster [quoted above as saying that the 'Jewish state' was never part of the Zionist programme] declared that what the Jews wish to obtain in Palestine was not merely a right to establish colonies, or educational, cultural or industrial institutions. They wanted to establish in Palestine an autonomous Jewish commonwealth in the fullest sense of the word. They wanted Palestine to be Palestine *of* the Jews, and not merely a Palestine *for* Jews. They wished the land again to be what it was in olden times and what it had been for Jews in their prayers and in their Bible — a land of Israel. The ground must be theirs."[44]

"The fact came out repeatedly in the Commission's conferences with Jewish representatives that the Zionists looked forward to a practically complete dispossession of the present non-Jewish inhabitants of Palestine."[45]

"Soon after the Biltmore conference in New York in May 1942, Ben-Gurion reiterated his commitment for a 'Jewish state' in all of historic Palestine. He explained in a meeting of Histadrut Counsel: 'this is why we formulated our demand *not as a Jewish state in Palestine but Palestine as a Jewish state*' (emphasis added), and he advised 'not to identify the Biltmore Program with a Jewish state in part of Palestine.'" [46]

General Patrick Hurley, personal representative of President Roosevelt in the Middle East reported: "For its part, the Zionist Organization in Palestine has indicated its commitment to an enlarged program for: (1) A sovereign Jewish state which would embrace Palestine and probably Transjordania[sic]; (2) An eventual transfer of the Arab population from Palestine to Iraq; and (3) Jewish leadership for the whole Middle East in the fields of economic development and control."[47]

ARTHUR KOESTLER: "There is surely neither hope nor meaning in a Jewish National Home unless we are prepared to let Jews ... enter this tiny land in such numbers as to become the majority ... Let the Arabs be encouraged to move out, as the Jews move in. ... The Arabs have many wide territories of their own; they must not claim to exclude the Jews from this small area of Palestine, less than the size of Wales. Indeed, we should re-examine also the possibility of extending the present Palestinian boundaries, by agreement with Egypt, Syria or Transjordan."[48]

I apologise if all these quotes are overegging the pudding but throughout this book I am trying to fight fire with fire. Since, with every opportunity, Israel and its supporters swamp the media with false accounts of the history of the conflict, these need to be countered with a similar weight of evidence. To counter a battery of denials that the Zionists wanted to turn Palestine into a Jewish state by quoting one Zionist as admitting that he clearly did, might seem as if I had cherry-picked a quote that suited my purpose. And even the

30

statements I quote are a small subset of what is available to make the same point.

As Britain took over control of Palestine and set up an administration to run the country 'in the interests of all its inhabitants', many Palestinians still could not believe that Britain and the Zionists were lying about the Jewish 'National Home,' still less that the facts were deliberately being concealed from them *by British officials*. But they were. Richard Meinertzhagen, a pro-Zionist British officer in the military administration in Jerusalem, wrote to his boss, the Foreign Secretary, Lord Curzon:

> "The people of Palestine are not at present in a fit state to be told openly that the establishment of Zionism in Palestine is the policy to which H.M.G., America and France are committed. They certainly do not realise this fact. It has therefore been found advisable to withhold for the present your telegram No. 245 of August 4th, 1919, from general publication. So soon as Dr. Weizmann arrives, I intend to draw up with him and the Chief Administrator a statement giving in the most moderate language what Zionism means: the gradual manner of its introduction, its freedom from religious or industrial intolerance, its eventual benefits to Palestine, and the denial that immigration spells the flooding of Palestine with the dregs of Eastern Europe."[49]

(Meinertzhagen's 'moderate' statement of what Zionism means is, of course, itself a tissue of lies.)

The way Meinertzhagen's prejudices clouded his judgment is best shown by another remark to Lord Curzon in 1919:

> "My conviction that anti-Zionist feeling is largely artificial and has been exaggerated both locally and at home is more than ever confirmed on further investigation. I do not anticipate any serious trouble in the initial stages of Zionism with the present moderation displayed by Zionist leaders."[50]

But then this is a man who wrote in his diary after Germany was defeated in the First World War, "Germany has learned her lesson, and I see no reason why she should not for the future be one of the leading moral lights in the family of Nations."[51]

Every Palestinian knew of his own long history in the land, the social and demographic roots that underlay the communities Palestinians lived in, and the structures of local government, trade, transport, and agriculture that had built up over generations, and they could not understand how a group of European Jews could believe for a moment that it would be possible to achieve such a radical transformation. Unfortunately, as the 1920s became the 1930s it became only too apparent that, initially with the help of the British and then in conflict with them, Zionism was gaining footholds in all aspects of the administration of Palestine. It didn't diminish these anxieties that the British Colonial Secretary in the 1920s, Winston Churchill, was a Zionist, and that the first High Commissioner of Palestine, Herbert Samuel, the leading administrative figure, was a Jew as well as a Zionist. He was one of three candidates for the job, and Palestinian anxieties might have been even greater if the Palestinians had known that all three candidates were nominated by the Zionist Organisation.

One under-appreciated aspect of the way in which Palestine was lost to Zionism is the role played by a man we have heard a bit about already, Dr. Chaim Weizmann, leader of the Zionist Organisation. The 19th century historian Thomas Carlyle stated that "The History of the world is but the Biography of great men." Setting aside the adjective 'great', I think there is no doubt that the history of Palestine would have been very different without the part played by Weizmann. At every turn, from 1917 to 1947, this man wielded an influence on the British government and the civil administration in Palestine which thwarted every attempt by Britain to be even-handed between the Arabs of Palestine and the Jews.

His manoeuvres were played out behind the scenes, in Chelsea drawing rooms and Whitehall offices or through chummy personal letters to senior British figures, and were usually at great variance with his public statements, which always dismissed the idea – perish the thought! – that Zionist participation in Palestine would ever harm the rights or fortunes of the majority Arab population.

It is galling to read the voluminous, once secret, archives setting out the years of discussions between the British government, the British administrators in Palestine, the Zionists and the occasional Arab delegations which tried to get their case heard. They reveal that while the Zionists were presented in public as reasonable partners with the British government in planning the way forward in Palestine, Weizmann was often as infuriating to the British as to the Palestinians. While the British tried to allay the fears among the Palestinians of a Jewish takeover, they were tearing their hair out as the Zionists, and particularly Weizmann, sabotaged the message. What is more, the British ministers and civil servants didn't always agree with each other, and the pro-Zionists among them would pass on to Weizmann information about government plans or cabinet discussions.

Balfour himself seemed unable to believe that he was being lied to by Weizmann, as Lord Curzon, the Foreign Secretary during the Peace Talks tried to point out to him:

> "I feel tolerably sure therefore that while Weizmann may say one thing to you, or while you may mean one thing by a National Home, he is out for something quite different. He contemplates a Jewish State, a Jewish nation, a subordinate population of Arabs etc. ruled by Jews; the Jews in possession of the fat of the land, and directing the Administration. He is trying to effect this behind the screen and under the shelter of British trusteeship [i.e. the League of Nations Mandate]. I do not envy those who wield the latter, when they realise the pressure to which they are certain to be exposed…"[52]

A later memo between two senior civil servants in the Colonial Office highlighted the sort of conflicts which were bedevilling the plans for Palestine:

> "The Zionist Organisation, in the person of Dr. Weizmann, enjoys direct access to high political personages outside the Colonial Office. Doctor Weizmann told me recently that he had

asked the Prime Minister orally not very long ago, what meaning His Majesty's Government had attached to the phrase 'Jewish National Home' in the famous Balfour Declaration. The Prime Minister replied: 'We meant a Jewish State'. I do not know what may have been the original intention, but it was certainly the object of Sir Herbert Samuel and the Secretary of State, to make it clear that a Jewish State was just what we did *not* mean. It is clearly useless for us to endeavour to lead Doctor Weizmann in one direction, and to reconcile him to a more limited view of the Balfour pledge, if he is told quite a different story by the head of the government.   Nothing but confusion can result if His Majesty's Government do not speak with a single voice."[53]

While the British government was trying to present a stance of even-handedness to a delegation of Palestinian Arabs, Weizmann seems to have behaved like a bull in a china shop, displaying all the contempt for the Arabs we have seen already among the Zionists. As another Colonial Office civil servant commented on a meeting he had attended:

"Dr. Weizmann, while his speech was conciliatory, adopted an unfortunate manner in delivering it. His attitude was of the nature of a conqueror handing to beaten foes the terms of peace. Also I think he despises the members of the delegation as not worthy protagonists - that it is a little derogatory to him to expect him to meet them on the same ground. It seems to me that it is quite hopeless to expect Arabs and Zionists to meet on common ground when that ground is already occupied by His Britannic Majesty's Government on the Balfour Declaration, no matter what be the interpretation of that Declaration and no matter in what forms its substance is embodied..."[54]

Much of the internal correspondence suggests that the Colonial Office officials were actually afraid of Weizmann and his Zionist colleagues and were more interested in mollifying him than dealing with the rights of the Palestinians. One civil servant wrote:

"It is quite certain that the Jewish National Home policy will go to blazes if we break with the Zionist Organisation, and I think equally certain that, if we force Dr W into too difficult a position, he will either leave the Z[ionist] O[rganisation], which would be disastrous to the whole policy, or go over to the extremists and break with us."[55]

The Chief Secretary to the Palestine government, Wyndham Deedes, a man who had to deal on a daily basis in Palestine with the effect on the Palestinian Arabs of the tussle between the Zionists and the Colonial Office wrote to his superiors in London:

"It seemed to everyone so absurd that a Body like the Zionist Organisation, officially recognized by H.M.G. for certain purposes should continue to express views diametrically opposed to those of the Government that had accorded it recognition... H.M.G's recent Declaration of Policy was declared by the Zionist Organisation to be wholly inacceptable, a Betrayal, and much else of that nature.

The Arab population waited to see what would happen, to see which would indeed prove to be the Predominant Partner in the Association.

Would H.M.G. insist upon the Zionists accepting the Government Policy, and if they refused to do so would H.M.G. sever their connexion with the Zionists?

People waited in vain. Nothing happened. What deductions could the Arabs draw from all this?

They could draw but the one they did - that H.M.G. was bound hand and foot to the Zionists, and that all Legislation here was and would continue to be inspired by Zionist Interests."[56]

If there were any doubt about the British politicians who were responsible for Palestine being in thrall to the Zionists, it should be dispelled by the following extract from a secret note in Zionist archives. It describes a dinner in London in 1937, at the height of Palestinian discontent over the growing influence in Palestine of the Jewish Agency. Weizmann attended, along with two former Colonial Secretaries, Winston Churchill and Leo Amery:

"Note of conversation at dinner given by Sir Archibald Sinclair, 1 Thorney Court London W8 on Tuesday 8th of June 1937 at 8:30 pm

Present: Sir Archibald Sinclair, Mr Winston Churchill, Mr Amery, Mr Atlee, Colonel Wedgewood, Captain Casalet, Mr James de Rothschild, Dr Weizmann

The conversation after dinner was largely monopolised by Mr Churchill ...

Mr Churchill ... said to Dr Weizmann: You know, you are our master – and yours, and yours (pointing to other members of the party) - and what you say goes. If you ask us to fight we will fight like tigers."[57]

With no one in the British or Palestine governments willing to face up to Weizmann, it is not surprising that over the major issues that troubled the Palestinian Arabs, it was the Zionists who made the running every time.

Although the Palestinian Arabs were in the majority in their country for the entire period of the Mandate, the Zionists set up the Jewish Agency to ensure that the much smaller Jewish population of Palestine received preferential treatment at the expense of the Arab community. The Agency also pressured the British to permit immigration of Jews to Palestine in large numbers, in an effort to increase the *quantitative* predominance of Jews in addition to the qualitative predominance they proclaimed for themselves.

It was this regular influx of Jews, granted immediate citizenship of Palestine, that helped to reinforce an awareness among Palestinians that the unthinkable might occur – the loss of freedom in the land their families had lived in for generations.

Chapter 4: Zionism at work

"Palestine has been Zionised. ... [W]e have the High Commissioner himself, we have the High Commissioner's son, who is, I think, one of the Assistant Governors of Jerusalem, the Legal Secretary is a Zionist, the Director of Commerce and Industry is a Zionist, the Director of Central Stores is a Zionist, the Director of Labour is a Zionist, the Assistant Director of Public Security, the Assistant Director of Railways and Traffic Manager, the Assistant Director of Emigration at Jaffa, the Director of Emigration at Haifa, the District Engineer at Haifa, the District Engineer at Jaffa, the Director of Companies Registration, the Senior Quarantine Officer at Jaffa, the Assistant Public Custodian at Haifa, are all of them Jews and Zionists."

Sir W. Joynson-Hicks, M.P. House of Commons debate, 4th July, 1922

In 1906, in Tsarist St Petersburg, a Russian Orthodox priest, Father Georgy Apollonovich Gapon, was invited by a friend to a cottage outside the city. The friend was a man called Pinchas Rutenberg, a Zionist Jew, who had set up the meeting in order to murder Gapon. Rutenberg was a friend in the sense that he had once saved Gapon's life after police attacks on a demonstration in support of workers' rights, helping him to flee and change into peasants' clothing. But a year later, after discovering that Gapon was working as a police informer, Rutenberg and three colleagues murdered him.

Rutenberg's name acquired considerable notoriety in the years leading up to the coming into force of the British Mandate over Palestine, not because he was a murderer but because, as part of the long-term Zionist plan for Palestine, he was given an extraordinarily broad-ranging contract to provide electricity and other public services for Palestine. In a debate in 1922 about this contract, known as the Rutenberg Concession, and whether the British government had the right to award it, Winston Churchill, then Colonial Secretary, said – charitably, I would say – "I have no doubt that his [Rutenberg's] record is one which would not in every respect compare with that of those who have been fortunate enough to live their lives in this settled and ordered country." So that's all right then.

The issue, which became a *cause celebre* during the early years of the Mandate, was twofold. First, when the Rutenberg contract was awarded, Britain had not been officially granted control of Palestine. Because of that, other industrial contractors – both British and Arab – who wanted to bid for utilities had been firmly told by the Colonial Office that their proposals could not be considered until all the details of Britain's mandate had been settled. In fact, as far back as 1916, the Zionists had laid before the British Cabinet what was called the 'October programme' including a clause which said "in the event of Palestine coming under the control of England and of France" a Jewish Company was to be empowered "to acquire for its own use all or any concessions which may at anytime be granted by the suzerain Government or Governments." As a result, Pinchas Rutenberg and his engineers had begun drawing up plans for what was to be an entirely Jewish-controlled electrification and industrialisation of Palestine.

J.M.N. Jeffries, a *Daily Mail* journalist, wrote scathingly about the lack of any pressing need for such a major project:

> "[N]o Chief Administrator of Palestine during the O.E.T.A.*
> period had looked over the country on arrival and cried, 'The
> Jordan calls imperatively for damming. The electric current must
> be obtained for want of which the land is perishing.' The land
> could have done with electric current in Haifa, Jerusalem, Jaffa
> and, say, Nablus, but it could have done without it just as well.
> Probably of Tel-Aviv alone might it be said that there was real
> need for more light upon it. In general there was no noticeable
> public outcry for electric current, though some Arabs had it in
> mind. They would have provided it more suitably for most
> towns by local powerhouse schemes. Nazareth and Tiberias
> were lit already by such local schemes, and the principal
> buildings in Jerusalem had their own plants."[58]

---

* Occupied Enemy Territory Administration – the postwar, pre-Mandate
administration in Palestine.

Clearly, once the League of Nations granted control of Palestine to Britain, there would be a lot of opportunities for improving public services and utilities in the country, and there were plenty of other contractors who were happy to put forward schemes. Sir W. Joynson-Hicks, M.P. explained in the Commons debate how a number of proposals from round the world had been turned down, and he mentioned the runaround given to one particular British engineer, Mr Bicknall:

"Just at the end of the war he put forward a scheme to the British Overseas Trade Department for the development of certain minerals and electric schemes in Palestine, and the Overseas Trade Department was so keenly in favour of this scheme that it promised to support it. ... [But] on the 4th May, 1920, he received a reply stating that, pending a settlement of the future status of that country at the conclusion of a Treaty of Peace with Turkey, no concessions could be made. After that, he went again to the Overseas Department, and he was told that all his papers had been sent out to Palestine. He then went to the Zionist organisation, and he was astonished to find that they knew all about the scheme and all about his plans, and he has had no reply at all from the Government of Palestine as to this scheme, part of which is now embodied in the Rutenberg contract."[59]

There were also Arab industrialists who had proposals for the type of work laid out in the Rutenberg plans:

"In 1920 the Deputy-Governor of Bethlehem put up a scheme by two very rich Christian Arabs, Messrs. Hanna Dabdoud and Handel, great South American merchants, for part of what Rutenberg has got, namely, a concession for electric lighting and power supply in Jerusalem and district, for the agricultural development of the Jordan Valley, and a motor transport service. These are Christian Arabs, and the Deputy-Governor stated to the Government that they were prepared to begin with half a million of money themselves and that they were able to control £2,000,000. That was put up by the Deputy-Governor, and the reply was received that no concessions could be given pending the granting of a mandate. ... Even the Jaffa municipality itself asked for a concession for the use of the Auja river, which is part of the Rutenberg concession, for the electric lighting of their own town and district, and that was again turned down by the Government."[60]

Churchill's anti-Arabism, even if he had not been in thrall to the Zionists, would have meant the kiss of death for the proposals of the two Christian Arabs, however rich. In the House of Commons debate, he said:

"I am told that the Arabs would have done it themselves. Who is going to believe that? Left to themselves, the Arabs of Palestine would not in a thousand years have taken effective steps towards the irrigation and electrification of Palestine. They would have been quite content to dwell—a handful of philosophic people—in the wasted sun-scorched plains, letting the waters of the Jordan continue to flow unbridled and unharnessed into the Dead Sea."[61]

Presumably, Churchill, if he had lived long enough, would have been astonished to see that the 22 member countries of the Arab League all have electric light and hot and cold running water.

In fact, the Arabs had applied on various occasions to set up proper irrigation projects. They had applied for local electrifications: they had asked for concessions based on agriculture. But this had been denied by the Colonial Office under Churchill. As Jeffries writes, "He spoke scornfully of the Arabs for their never attempting what he, as head of his Department, never allowed them to try."

The Rutenberg scheme was granted unbelievably advantageous conditions which were never offered to other companies. These included loans on entirely non-commercial terms, a 70-year lifetime for the contract, and extensive tax concessions, as well as rights of compulsory purchase of land and buildings. One M.P. Sir J. Butcher, was astonished at the privileges Rutenberg had been given.

"To put this Palestine company into a perfectly impregnable position, the High Commissioner binds himself and all his successors to the end of the 70 years, or whatever time the concession may be extended, to expropriate for the benefit of this company any existing undertakings for the generation and supply of electricity in the whole of the area of Palestine. He goes further and binds himself, upon the bare request of the company, to expropriate any individual from his land, his buildings and his property, which are to be handed over to the company ... But that is not the legislation to which we are accustomed in this country, that you should give the power to the concessionaire on the one hand, and an unknown person, who may be High Commissioner at some future date, to expropriate every individual from his land, buildings and property at their own sweet will. Is that fair to the inhabitants of Palestine, or to the interests of the Arabs? If that is how you preserve the rights of the Arabs in your Mandate, it is a novel Mandate. It is unknown outside of Palestine."[62]

The scheme was presented by Churchill in the Commons debate as an "irrigation scheme", as if it was largely an agricultural project, which might be seen as helping Arab farmers. But according to Jeffries this was far from its actual purpose:

"In the clauses [of the Contract] ... the aim of the Rutenberg scheme was made manifest. To provide current to 'factories, works and undertakings,' to 'set up and carry on factories, works and undertakings' —that was the goal of the scheme. Its devisers meant to make of Palestine a land of industrialism, linked with the centres of industrialism about the globe.

It is true that this seems in flagrant contradiction with their most advertised intention, that of restoring the Jewish people to contact with the soil, by agricultural work. But agricultural work has never appealed to more than a small minority of the Zionist public. Most of that public has never had the faintest intention of taking to the cultivation of the soil, were Palestine as fertile as the Ukraine and as empty as the Sahara. The Zionist bodies and the Zionist press-agents, of course, have always seen to it that newspapers everywhere have been supplied with attractive pictures of sunburnt young Jewish haymakers, and the Zionist orators have always supplied equally attractive word-pictures of the same hay makers to countless meetings and discussions. But the real emblem of the National Home should be a clerical worker or a shopkeeper at his Tel-Aviv counter. More than three-quarters of the Jewish population is, and always has been ... far from the land. It congregates in towns and in urban areas which are becoming yearly more distended. The Zionists nominally fled from cities and towns, but once in Palestine they started to build them with every sign of glee.

To great engineering firms the industrialization of a small place such as Palestine, and the mastery of Palestine's resources, presented no attraction, for they gave no prospect of high dividends within a reasonable period. But they meant everything to the Zionists, whose aim at this stage was to master Palestine, whether it paid or not, to turn it into a business-land, whether the business were good or not."[63]

None of the protests or criticisms of the Rutenberg scheme had any effect on the British administration, even though the various projects included in the Concession sometimes cast a blight on the Arabs' own efforts, denigrated by Churchill.

A number of Arabs in Haifa wanted to build and operate a power station but they were told they had to ask the Rutenberg Company for permission to light their own town. The municipal council of Tulkarm applied to the Governor for permission to do something similar. It too was told to apply to Rutenberg. "Very properly they refused to do so," Jeffries writes, "and decided to abide as long as they could by the oil-lamps of their fathers."

In 1920, a former British soldier formed an Anglo-Arab group to reclaim malarial marshes for cultivation. He was refused, on the grounds that no concessions could be given till the Mandate was ratified. The next he heard was that the Rutenberg Concessions had been granted, even though the Mandate was still not ratified.

The Rutenberg Concession provides a major illustration of how early the Zionist movement had begun to collude with the British government to create the conditions that favoured a Western-oriented Jewish state, rather than allowing for the culturally and politically appropriate development of the majority community in Palestine, the Palestinian Arabs. It was also the cause of friction among Arab workers who were often denied work on Rutenberg Projects because of a Jewish labour unions policy of 'Jewish labour for Jewish land'.

The growing industrialisation of Palestine, often favouring Jewish towns and communities, was accompanied by Zionist pressure on the Administration to allow increased Jewish immigration to Palestine.

Pinchas Rutenberg in one of his power stations.

Immigration of foreigners is a thorny issue in many countries at the moment. Some people are against any immigration at all to their country, sometimes for nationalistic or racist reasons; others see immigration as having a mix of good and bad consequences for a country, and still others see it as entirely beneficial. One benefit for a country like the United Kingdom is the rectification of shortages in occupations which British people are unwilling or unable to fill.

The issue of Jewish immigration to Palestine in the period from 1920 to 1947 presented different issues to the Palestinian people from those addressed in 21st century Britain. Today, as the boats empty their passengers on to Kent shores, no asylum seeker is saying "We have come here in the hope of forming a government in a few years' time and preventing you exercising your political rights." Nor did the Palestinians feel a racist attitude towards Jews. There were Jews already in Palestine, in small numbers, many of whose families had lived there for generations, in traditional centres of Judaism such as Jerusalem, Haifa, Safad and Tiberias. There were also idealistic Jewish pioneers, many of them socialists, who isolated themselves in kibbutzim and on farms. Relations between Arabs and Jews when they lived in mixed communities were usually cordial. It was the ill-concealed wishes of Zionist Jews to take over control of Palestine that led to Palestinian fears of Jewish immigration. And the Palestinians certainly saw no countervailing advantage, such as Jews filling jobs which Palestinians wouldn't or couldn't fill. Apart from anything else, when Jews began to immigrate to Palestine, they congregated together, set up their own communities and enterprises, and played no part in the traditional life and activities of the Palestinian Arab community.

It's not difficult to put oneself in the shoes of Palestinians, faced with regular and increasing numbers of foreign, i.e. Jewish, immigrants to Palestine. And the word 'foreign' is the appropriate one to use here. Jews formed less than ten percent of the population at the time of the Balfour Declaration. The vast majority of Jews who came to Palestine in several waves of immigration from Europe between the 1920s and 1940s had no family or ethnic connection with Palestine and, indeed, did not participate in the society and culture of Palestine.

The writer Arthur Koestler, who observed his fellow-Jews, all Europeans, as they arrived in Palestine, commented on how they studiously avoided any kind of assimilation into what was an oriental country.

> "The Jews made no effort to bring European culture to the Arab masses, nor to adapt themselves to those aspects of oriental life which would have enriched their own cultural pattern and at the same time made them appear less provocatively alien to the

country. They did not learn from the Arabs to build cool and spacious houses which would fit the climate and landscape; they brought with them their architecture of the Polish small town and of German functionalism of the 'twenties. Their dress, food, manners and general way of life were transplanted like a prefabricated pattern from their lands of origin. Some of these were improvements in the country's way of life; others unfitting and in bad taste. There was no cultural symbiosis between the two races. The Jews came as conquerors. It was a fair and humane conquest, but a conquest nevertheless."[64]

Before we get too dewy-eyed about Koestler's apparent philo-Arabism, it is worth quoting another remark from the same work, describing an imagined scene after a Jewish takeover of Palestine:

"A few weeks later some Arab lads will start sniping from these villages at Jewish trucks on the road; the Jewish army will herd the villagers together, dynamite their houses, and put the young men into concentration camps; while the old ones will tie a mattress and a brass coffee-pot on the donkey, the old woman will walk ahead leading the donkey by the rein and the old man will ride on it, wrapped in his kefiye, and sunk in solemn meditation about the lost opportunity of raping his youngest grandchild."[65]

In the case of Jewish immigration to Palestine, at least in the first years of the Mandate, there were none of the 'push' factors that apply in modern waves of immigration. It wasn't usually a matter of desperate people fleeing their homes to find a safe haven in Palestine. That became one of the factors later, as antisemitism in Eastern Europe and the Nazi persecution of Jews took its vicious hold, although as I show in a later chapter, many Jews fleeing the antisemitic persecution wanted to go to the US, Canada, or other European countries, rather than the hot, dry, 'uncivilised' country of Palestine.

The true 'push factors' for the early waves of Jewish immigration to Palestine were political. Under the League of Nations Mandate, Britain was to be responsible for implementing the Balfour Declaration through negotiations with "an appropriate Jewish Agency ... by facilitating Jewish immigration ... and encouraging close settlement on the land." And the Zionists never ceased to pressure the British, if they felt the figures for immigration permits were too low.

As Britain began to realise that it had to choose between the two commitments in the Balfour Declaration – a Jewish state or the rights of the indigenous population, it was the Palestinians' rights that went by the board. Internal battles between the Zionists and the Colonial Office were usually lost by the government and over a period of fifteen years the *Yishuv*, or Jewish community in Palestine, grew by about 80 per cent, the high point for immigration coming in 1935, when 62,000 persons entered Palestine.

By 1936, Jews made up about 28% of the population of Palestine, still far below the quantitative superiority they desired, but nevertheless an increasing threat to the daily lives of the Palestinian population. The Palestinians had been reassured by the government that Jewish immigration would be permitted only up to what was called the 'economic absorptive capacity' of the country, a rather vague concept which was ignored by the Zionists pressuring the government to increase the numbers.

In any case, the rules were pretty loose. Legal immigrants could bring relatives, provided they were not of an age to enter the labour market, a rule often ignored. Any person with a capital of £1000 could become an immigrant. Students and religious professions were automatically granted permission, and many immigrants registered at the Hebrew University but never attended a class. Young women arrived declaring fictitious marriages to Jews already there.

When the issue of illegal immigration to Palestine was discussed in the British parliament, Lloyd George dismissed such worries: "There is criticism of the Jews because some of them went there temporarily and remained, attracted by the country."

Nevill Barbour, an English writer who lived in Palestine in the 1930s, was scathing about the laxity of control over Jews coming to Palestine:

"The writer of these pages well remembers his arrival in Palestine in the autumn of 1933. I travelled from Istanbul to Haifa in a Bulgarian ship which also carried several hundred steerage passengers. These were Rumanian and Bulgarian Jews, who, on my asking where they were going and what they were doing, told me, to my astonishment, that they were 'tourists going to visit Palestine. Of course, if the country attracts us,' they said, using, no doubt unconsciously, the very words of Mr Lloyd George, 'we may remain.' On arrival at Haifa the 'tourists' marched ashore in their hundreds without encountering any difficulties from the immigration authorities. Hundreds more who had not even a tourist visa landed secretly by night on lonely portions of the coast."[66]

What riled the Palestinians was not just the increasing competition for jobs and land, but the inflammatory statements of some Zionists about the purposes of this immigration, to give eventual control of the country to its Jews. While such statements would be denied by the British, they contained wild and worrying forecasts.

"Towards the end of the current year there will be about 400,000 Jews in Palestine, (wrote one enthusiastic Zionist). By appropriate efforts it would be possible, within the five years 1936-40, to bring this figure to the potential number of 1,000,000 souls. This would require the immigration during this period of time of 150,000 young couples capable of breeding— that is to say, 30,000 couples annually, apart from old people and children."[67]

At the Zionist Congress of 1935 David Ben-Gurion, Chairman of the Jewish Agency Executive, "laid down a Zionist five-year plan for the immigration of 1,000,000 families, five million people altogether. The whole Middle East, as Ben-Gurion saw it, was destined to be the stage of the new Jewish renaissance."[68]

Since 1917, anti-Arab racism and the lying that accompanied it had already alerted the Palestinian population to a threat they initially had thought unrealisable. Now the evidence of growing immigration, accompanied by the overt intention to make Palestine a Jewish state, showed that the threat was genuine.

A related cause for anxiety and anger was the relentless and unjust preference given by the British to the Jewish community in Palestine at the expense of the Palestinian Arabs. It was no coincidence that the only reference to Palestinian rights in the Balfour Declaration was to 'civil and religious rights' of the 'non-Jewish' inhabitants. The one thing the Zionists were unwilling to see granted to the Palestinians was *political* rights – the right of self-determination and participation in the government of their own country.

As the numbers of Jews increased in Palestine, their claims for preferential treatment at the expense of the Arabs grew louder. A Jewish socialist who tried to live by his principles, described how, when he got to Palestine he was compelled to breach them:

> "[In Palestine] I had to fight my friends on the issue of Jewish socialism, to defend the fact that I would not accept Arabs in my trade union, the Histadrut; to defend preaching to the [Jewish] housewives that they not buy at Arab stores, to prevent Arab workers from getting jobs there. .... To pour kerosene on the Arab tomatoes; to attack Jewish housewives in the markets and smash the Arab eggs they had bought; to praise to the skies the *Keren Kayemet* [Jewish National Fund] that sent [Jews] to Beirut to buy land from absentee landlords and to throw the fellahin off the land. To buy dozens of dunums [dunum=.25 acre] from an Arab is permitted, but to sell, God forbid, one Jewish dunum to an Arab is prohibited."[69]

The land issue was central to the Jewish attempt to take over Palestine. Even by 1947, twenty years after the Balfour Declaration, Jews would legally own only 6% of the land in Palestine. But they had found all sorts of illicit ways to obtain land against the best interests of its Arab owners, as another Jewish resident with a guilty conscience said:

> "I realized how serious the issue of our relations with the Arabs is when I first purchased lands from the Arabs (In the Galilee) ... I realized how close the Bedouin is to his land... During my 25 years of colonial work I have dispossessed many Arabs from their lands, and you understand that this job – of dispossessing people from the land in which they and maybe their father were born – is not at all an easy thing, especially when one looks at these people as human beings ... I had to do this, because this is what the *Yishuv* asked for, but I always tried to do it in the best way possible... I got familiar with the Arabs and the Arab question very early on." [70]

(This is a good example of an Israeli ethos described by anti-Zionist Israeli, Ilan Pappé as "shoot and cry.")

In other Middle East countries that had been freed from Ottoman control after the War, steps were being taken towards self-determination. But in Palestine, the Jewish community and its supporters in London created a huge fuss whenever the British government made the smallest attempt to assuage Arab anxieties about the growing control of the *Yishuv* over the Palestinian administration. In particular, from early on in the Mandate, there had been a commitment by the British government to creating some kind of Legislative Council which, although only consultative, would give the appearance of participation of the Palestinians in their own affairs.

In 1922, a delegation of Palestinian Arabs visited London to express concerns about the Mandate and its possible consequences for the Palestinians, as laid out in a White Paper by the Colonial Secretary, Winston Churchill. Following a meeting with Churchill, the delegation wrote a letter expressing some concerns about various aspects of the White Paper, including a constitution for Palestine which included plans for a Legislative Council.

"We … hold that the proposed constitution is wholly unsatisfactory, because … Articles 17-28 dealing with the Legislative Council prescribe that this Council 'shall consist of 25 members in addition to the High Commissioner … who shall exercise a casting vote, in case of an equality of votes.' This brings the total number of votes to 27. Of these, 10 shall be official members holding office under the High Commissioner, and two members shall be nominated by him. Thus the High Commissioner commands 14 out of the 27 votes. Of the 12 elected members there will probably be 10 or 11 that would represent the Arab majority, who would be unable to carry any measure against the official preponderance of votes.

It is thus apparent that too much power is given to a High Commissioner whom we will suppose is impartial. But when, as is the case with the present High Commissioner, he is a Zionist, i.e. a member of the organisation which is prompting the flood of alien Jew immigration into Palestine, whose officials as well as those members appointed by him must, naturally, carry out his policy, and when one or two of the 12 elected members will most probably be Zionists, then the Zionist policy of the Government will be carried out under a constitutional guise, whereas at present it is illegal, against the rights and wishes of the people, and maintained by force of arms alone. … This invariably leads to the Executive becoming arbitrary since it is placed in the position of accused and judge at the same time.

We also notice with astonishment that 10 members constitute a quorum. This is less than half the total number of Members, and makes it possible for the 10 official members to carry on the work of legislation should circumstances, for any reason whatever, prevent the other members from being present. In which case the power of the Legislative Council becomes a mere shadow and not a reality."[71]

The delegation, made up of leading Christians and Moslems, saw that in such a Council, in any situation which might arise which the Arab members disagreed with, they could be outvoted by a combination of government members and Jews. The British refused to change the proposal and so the Arabs said they would boycott elections to such a Council.

Daily Mail reporter, J.M.N Jeffries wrote:

"The Zionists had affirmed enthusiastic adherence to the then proposed Legislative Council. They protested loudly then against the Government's condonation of the Arab boycott of the elections. The Jewish Press was indignant at the weakness of the Government and asked, 'Now that elections have been ordered by an Order in Council and that it was proclaimed that any one interfering with the elections would be prosecuted, why was this not carried out? Why was not the poisonous agitation stopped?"[72]

The Legislative Council proposal was shelved by the Palestine administration after the Arab boycott, since there was a lot more going on in Palestine which required its attention. In particular, friction grew between the indigenous Palestinian Arabs and the immigrant Jews who were starting to exert pressure on the local government for rights and privileges that would help implant a Jewish identity in the country alongside the Arab presence. The use of Hebrew on signs, Star of David flags flying, Hebrew on coins and stamps, all served to remind Palestinians that the Arab nature of their state was in danger of being deliberately diluted by the Zionist movement, as part of its pressure to turn Palestine into a Jewish state.

Outbreaks of violence between Arabs and Jews led to a government inquiry which criticized several provocative actions by the Zionist Organization, including a ban on Jews reselling land to Arabs and using Arab labourers on Jewish farms.

The constitution of the Jewish Agency signed at Zurich, August 14, 1929 actually spelled this out, saying:

"The land acquired shall be held as the inalienable property of the Jewish people. No Arab can ever purchase it again. A provision to this effect is incorporated in every lease. ... In all the works and undertakings carried out or furthered by this Agency it shall be deemed to be a matter of principle that Jewish labor shall be employed."[73]

The government inquiry also called for stricter controls to be placed on Jewish immigration, and asserted—for the first time—that the British government had obligations "of equal weight" to both communities and that it must renew the effort to establish the Legislative Council.

The Palestinian Arabs thought that, at last, someone was listening to their grievances. That someone was Lord Passfield – formerly Sidney Webb – who, as Colonial Secretary wrote a White Paper which for once recognized how much Zionist pressure there had been on previous Colonial Secretaries to favour the Jews in Palestine over its indigenous population at every turn.

Looking back, it is astonishing to see the way in which the Zionists had access to the inner corridors of power in London, when the Palestinian Arabs could only read in the newspapers – after the events – about the decisions that were taken about their future. It was helped of course by the shuttle 'diplomacy' of Chaim Weizmann and his colleagues, one month in Palestine, another at home in London.

To see how he operated, one example will represent all. When Lord Passfield became Colonial Secretary, Weizmann sought an interview and left him in no doubt about how the British government should behave:

> "The Government ought to be clear on the point that we were not interested in building up a country for the Arabs, and to play a role similar to that, say, played by the Germans in Czechoslovakia ... our conception of the Jewish National Home was that of a great Jewish settlement. To that end we should seek to pack as many Jews into Palestine as was at all possible." [74]

Weizmann also told Passfield the names of two British civil servants in Palestine whom he felt to be pro-Arab (or not Zionist enough) and wanted removed:

> "For reasons which are self-evident, I feel regretfully obliged to request that His Majesty's Government may consider the propriety of relieving Mr. Luke and Mr. Cust of their duties..." [75]

(As far as (Colonel) Cust was concerned, HMG presumably considered and rejected the propriety of relieving him of his duties, because he remained a member of the Palestine Civil Service for another six years. Mr. Luke continued as deputy High Commissioner for some time and then was made Governor of Malta in 1930.)

One can imagine Weizmann's outrage when Passfield carried out the brief he had been given – to suggest a way forward in Palestine in the light of growing violence and conflict between Arabs and Jews. In fact, we don't need to imagine it. This is what Weizmann wrote to a fellow Zionist when Passfield's White Paper was published:

"He is no doubt a difficulty. His attitude is that it is his role to protect the poor Arabs against the powerful Jews. ... Passfield seems to be frightened and seems to assume the role of the patron saint of the Arabs. He is a tired old man; the whole thing came just at the beginning of his governmental career: one can reason and argue with him but he is rather obstinate."[76]

The British government seemed to have acquired a backbone for a time following Passfield's White Paper. After a series of attempts to change government policy, with long lists of pro-Zionist proposals from the Zionists which were rejected by the British government, Weizmann threw a hissy fit and resigned as President of the Jewish Agency and the Zionist Organisation.

The government of Palestine came under the Colonial Office, whom the Zionists blamed for all the 'pro-Arab' (really 'pro-Mandate') recommendations and the Jewish Agency plotted to ensure that control was taken away from that department and handed to the Foreign Office which they saw as more pro-Zionist.

"If that is done," wrote the Agency's secretary, "we shall deal with infinitely more intelligent officials ... with men of a wider view than the rather parochial C.O. officials and more accessible to influence from America and Geneva."[77]

The Zionists were also dismissive of the calibre of civil servants sent out by the British government to Palestine:

"British officials in Palestine were, as a rule, recruited from the ranks of the colonial service, which, generally speaking, did not make for great vision or imagination. ...Used to dealing with natives, they temperamentally preferred the primitive, and sometimes the picturesque, Arab to the Jew, who was more argumentative because conscious of his rights and, what was worse, considered himself their equal."[78]

While all these events might seem like ancient history to us in the 21st century, the growing sense of powerlessness back then among ordinary Palestinians laid the seeds of today's conflict. Deprived of justice at every turn, outwitted and lied to by a more powerful adversary, there was a build-up of hostility among Palestinians against the Zionists, and against the British when they were seen to be ignoring the duty imposed upon them in the Mandate to facilitate 'the development of self-governing institutions'.

A gathering of senior Palestinians, in protest at the pro-Zionist activities of the British government.

Chapter 5: Despair sets in

It had not escaped the attention of literate Palestinians that as a result of the Peace Settlement after the Great War, other nations, some of them now freed of Ottoman control, were being ushered towards self-government along the lines laid down by President Wilson in his Fourteen Points Clearly, Palestinians deserved to be in a similar position to Iraqis or Egyptians, but because of the British promise to Zionists, they had to stand by and watch as Iraq and Egypt moved towards becoming independent self-ruling nations, while Palestinian claims of self-government were ignored.

From early on in relations between Zionists and the British government, Weizmann had made it clear that whatever Britain did about self-government for other Middle East countries, the Zionists would not accept any form of self-government for Palestine.

In July 1921, a group of senior government figures, including David Lloyd George, Prime Minister; Winston Churchill, Colonial Secretary; and Arthur Balfour, met Weizmann at Balfour's house. Notes made at the time show the grip that Weizmann had on the British government, and the unquestioning acceptance by the ministers of Weizmann's 'instructions' when the talk turned to self-government for two of the former Ottoman-controlled nations:

> "Churchill quoted Mesopotamia and Transjordan, to which Dr Weizmann replied, 'You will not convince me that self-government has been given to these two lands because you think it right; it has only been done because you must', to which Lloyd George, Balfour and Churchill all agreed.
>
> Dr. Weizmann: 'If you do the same thing with Palestine it means giving up Palestine – and that is what I want to know.'
>
> Lloyd George to Churchill: 'You mustn't give representative government to Palestine.'
>
> Churchill: 'I might have to bring it before the Cabinet.'
>
> Dr. W. said this was impossible."[79]

Such Zionist influence on His Majesty's Government went over the heads of the ordinary Palestinians, though the administration in Jerusalem was obviously aware of how its attempts to be fair, or not too unfair, to the Palestinians were being thwarted. When the government followed the Passfield recommendations and made a renewed offer to the Arabs of a Legislative Assembly, this was characterized by the Zionist press as "a policy of conciliating the Arab leaders at the expense of the Jewish National Home" and the Zionists made it clear that "the Jews would be unable to co-operate in any such Legislative Council," which they regarded as "untimely, dangerous, and likely to increase the plane of friction between the Arabs and the Jews."

As J.M.N Jeffries wrote at the time:

"The Zionist Congress reaffirmed blithely the reverse of what had been affirmed before [after Churchill's Legislative Council proposal], and Dr. Weizmann and his colleagues accordingly informed the High Commissioner that they rejected the scheme and had resolved to take no part in its operation. The Arabs, despite the intrinsic worthlessness of the proposed Council, were disposed to accept it without enthusiasm as a first instalment towards justice. In Mr. Churchill's 'Legislative Council' they would not have been allowed to speak of immigration. In the new 'Legislative Council' they at least would be allowed to speak of it, though no heed would be paid to what they would say."[80]

In fact, it suited neither the British nor the Zionists to have a genuinely representative Legislative Council, for two reasons. First, the last thing the government wanted was an assembly which could pass laws, or even object to laws already passed. In particular, a genuinely representative assembly might question the whole basis of the Jewish National Home which was seen as a central pillar of the Mandate.

The second reason that true democracy could not be allowed by the British to operate in Palestine is that the Zionists were vehemently opposed to it. In all their discussions with the government in London the Zionists insisted on *parity*, i.e. Jews would not be part of the Legislative Council unless they had an equal number of elected members to the Arabs. The idea of 'qualitative democracy' had not yet died. With the population figures as they were in the 1930s, the call for parity meant that, in Zionist eyes, a Jewish representative was clearly worth five Arabs.

As one historian puts it:

> "Zionist objections to the concept of immediate self-government were well-known at the colonial office. They argued that the standard of education and political experience of the population of Palestine did not make the experiment 'expedient or opportune'. As the mass of fellahin were illiterate and under the influence of a few effendis, any representative body based on such an electorate would be unfriendly both to British policy and the National Home." [81]

Of course, this argument conflates two separate issues. One, that the population of Palestine was not as educated or politically sophisticated as it might be, an issue which no other developed nation sees as an important argument against democracy, even though all populations have varying degrees of education. The other issue was the need for the Zionists to stack the pack so that on any issue, but particularly the issue of increasing the proportion of Jews in Palestine, the Zionist vote would always predominate.

Weizmann claimed in a later memoir that he had felt there had been a danger in pushing too hard against plans for a legislative council:

> "The position in which we placed ourselves by our refusal to consider the legislative council was ... an unfortunate one. The public heard the words 'legislative council for Palestine'; it heard of Zionist opposition; the obvious conclusion was that the Zionists were undemocratic or anti-democratic." [82]

(Well, yes.)

There were no lengths to which Zionist theoreticians would not go to argue against the demographic facts in

Palestine. Ze'ev Jabotinsky, who led a splinter Zionist group and who founded one of the Jewish terrorist groups we will learn about in later chapters, came up with a proposal which even outdid Harry Sacher's principle of 'qualitative democracy.'

In giving evidence to yet another of the many government inquiries, Jabotinsky promoted the idea that the *global Jewish population* should have representation in a Legislative Council:

> "That prominent expert, Mr. van Rees, was the first to say that, under the Mandate, 'the [whole] Jewish People have got to be considered as virtually inhabitants of Palestine.' After that you cannot create so-called representative institutions in which that larger partner, the Jewish people, is represented as a minority and the smaller partner, the population on the spot, is represented as a majority."[83]

Of course, most nations on Earth give votes only to people 'on the spot'. That's what democracy is, after all.

Wrangling over this issue was just one of many frustrations the Palestinians experienced during the 1930s. Along with Zionism's racism, the anti-Arab immigration policy, and now the refusal of Britain to consider genuine self-government, the pressure on Palestinians and the threat to the self-determination they had been promised increased. Because they did not have a representative body equivalent to the Jewish Agency with its access to government at all levels, the opportunities for Arabs to make their grievances felt were more limited, though that didn't stop them trying.

One incident among many gives an idea of the way the Zionists manipulated the system for their own ends. In 1935, there were 5,000 unemployed Jews in Palestine. This did not stop the Jewish Agency from applying for over 10,000 immigration permits, at the same time as pressuring the Palestine Administration to find jobs for the continuously arriving Jewish immigrants. As a result, unemployment increased among Arab workers, and the Arab Labour Federation protested about this. Then, in response to Zionist pressure, the government gave a contract to build three Arab schools in the Arab town of Jaffa to a Jewish contractor employing Jewish labour, and this provoked a letter from the Federation which gives some idea of the feelings of the Palestinian Arabs about the continuing discrimination against them in favour of the Jews in Palestine.

"February 11th, 1936:

I beg to draw your kind attention to the fact that giving the construction of the three school premises to a Jewish contractor who engaged only Jewish labourers was a subject of great sensation and protests among the Arab labourers who considered this act to be completely against their legal rights, for the following reasons:

1. The buildings are situated in an Arab area.

2. The government has never given a contract to an Arab in a Jewish area.

3. Arab labourers engaged in Jewish areas were dismissed by force in many cases.

4. Unemployment among the Arabs is very serious.

I believe that you will agree with me that the government should have studied the present psychological situation of the Arab labourers before signing such a contract which is forcing out their feelings since they are suffering terribly from the present economic crisis and are looking for any kind of work just to keep their families and themselves.

Lately, the labourers held several meetings, and I could feel that they are determined to have their full rights in these buildings, and I have been urged to request you to deal with this serious question and to give your final decision as soon as possible. I am also requested to inform you that my society is prepared to supply you with any number of labourers of any craft and at any time for this work and for any other work..."[84]

There is ample evidence of repeated official Arab protests to the British administration by Palestinians during the Mandate period, often written eloquently, movingly, and it should be said, politely, but even when the administration was sympathetic it was hidebound, either by the terms of the Mandate or by the much greater pressures from the growing Jewish community in Palestine.

One official inquiry said:

"There is no branch of the Administration with which the [Jewish] Agency does not concern itself … This powerful and efficient organization amounts, in fact, to a Government existing side by side with the Mandatory Government." [85]

Another described

"A virtual Jewish non-territorial State with its own executive and legislative organs, and even something in the nature of conscription to recruit its illegal armed forces." [86]

It was also a source of comment that many members of the Council of the Jewish Agency, its supreme governing body, neither "belonged" to Palestine nor lived there.

The Palestinian Arabs felt increasingly that they were faced with two enemies – the Zionists and the British. Having expected some kind of fair play from Britain when it was given the Mandate for Palestine in the 1920s, it became clear that the government was favouring the Jews over them at every turn. Jewish immigration doubled between 1931 and 1935, and a protest movement emerged, leading to strikes and demonstrations which the British suppressed. The continuing influence of Weizmann and his colleagues led some politicians and civil servants to warn of the imbalance this was causing between the political rights of Jews and Arabs in Palestine.

Guerrilla groups, led by Shaikh Iz al-Din al-Qassam, carried out vandalization and sabotage against the British, and his killing by British police caused outrage and calls for revolt against the British administration. At about the same time, a large shipment of smuggled arms was discovered at the port of Jaffa, leading to fears that a Jewish military takeover of Palestine was planned. Frustrated by the inability of Britain to control such Jewish activities, and the disruption of Arab farming, increasing rents, and unemployment, the Palestinians began a general strike followed by an armed insurrection which the British attempted to crush. This lasted for four years, leading to brutal attempts at suppression by the British army, and the deaths of perhaps a sixth of the adult male population.

A Muslim leader addresses Palestinian Arabs during the 1936 revolt.

During the Arab Revolt, as it was called, the main conflict was between Arabs and the British army, while the *Yishuv* quietly got on with expanding their activities and increasing illegal immigration.

The Revolt was eventually ended after the intervention of several other Arab states, but Britain could see that things could not be allowed to continue in this way, and, as usual, set up another Commission in 1937, under Lord Peel, to 'find a solution', as if one actually existed – like a new species of animal in the jungle – that just needed to be discovered by some kind of search party and which could square the circle of Britain's obligations under the Mandate.

The Jewish Agency had achieved so much in Palestine by the end of the 1930s, that on one interpretation of the phrase 'National Home' the aim had been achieved.

One English writer in Palestine wrote at the time:

"The [National] Home has prospered economically and culturally to an amazing degree. It has already become 'a centre in which the Jewish people as a whole may take, on grounds of religion and race, an interest and a pride.' They can and do. In his book *Thy Neighbour,* in 1936, Lord Melchett could write: 'Where our opponents prophesied failure, we have achieved triumph ... Nothing like it has ever been done before ... A miraculous development, one which any great Mediterranean power, France, Spain or Italy, would be proud to boast of.'

No wonder the Royal Commission of 1937 was able to say 'Today the National Home is a going concern.' In other words, the Jewish National Home *has* been established. ... The first half of the Balfour Declaration and the corresponding part of the Mandate, have been fulfilled."[87]

But of course, since a full transformation of Palestine into a Jewish state was what the Zionists intended from the very beginning, the fact that Palestinian Jews had achieved so much by the later 1930s was neither here nor there. The Jewish community in Palestine still fell far short of living in an entirely Jewish state, and the Zionists felt that more needed to be done to achieve this.

The report of the Peel Commission was issued on July 7th, 1937, and the idea it pulled out of a hat, it seemed, was to divide Palestine – as Caesar divided Gaul in the *Gallic Wars* – into three parts. It recommended that a Jewish state be set up in most of the coastal plain and the Galilee area, while Jerusalem, Bethlehem and a strip of land running to the sea between Tel Aviv and Jaffa was to be put under a permanent British mandate. What remained of the country would be attached to Transjordan, which would form an independent Arab state.

Nevill Barbour described the effect of these recommendations on both Jews and Arabs:

"In spite of the enthusiasm that the idea of a Jewish state aroused in the Jewish masses, it is certain that the idea of any kind of partition was a violent shock to Zionist opinion. Nevertheless, it immediately became clear that the majority of

62

official Zionist leaders considered that the formation of a Jewish state in part of Palestine and the setting up of a poverty-stricken and backward Arab state in its neighbourhood was the best, if not the only, method of eventually achieving the Zionist aim of a Jewish commonwealth in all Palestine." [88]

In fact, if Barbour had had access to the private correspondence of the Jewish leader David Ben-Gurion, he would have discovered that the Commission had not pulled the idea out of a hat. In fact, it wasn't even their idea, it was Ben-Gurion's, or so he claimed in a letter to a family member:

"At the beginning of February I summoned the Central Committee of the party. I addressed it on the grave fears I had about the Commission's proposals. ... we had to find a positive, radical solution. This could, I suggested, be in the direction of partitioning the country into two parts, so that in one part will arise a Jewish State ... and the other part would become an Arab state. ... I added: If this proposal comes from the Jewish side it is doomed. It must be presented as a British idea." [89]

The deeper one goes into Zionist archives the more one finds double- and treble-dealing. Comparing what Ben-Gurion wrote in private, above, to a letter from Weizmann to a leading American Zionist, Stephen Wise, we get a different view:

"Partition is not _my_ project; it never has been and never will be my project. It was sprung upon me in the last hour of the four secret sessions I had with the Commission. [90]

In fact, there was a pretence of accepting the idea of partition among some Zionists. Weizmann defended it to the 20th Zionist Congress in these terms, using a Talmudic saying:

"If the jug falls upon the stone, woe to the jug. If the stone falls upon the jug, woe to the jug." [91]

Anyone in Palestine who had clung to the idea that justice would prevail and there would eventually be an Arab state of Palestine, just as there was an Arab state of Iraq, and soon to be an Arab state of Syria, surely gave up hope when they read

Peel's partition proposal. This was a dog's dinner of elements, including Jewish areas inhabited by thousands of Arabs, a corridor from Jerusalem to Jaffa that would remain in British hands, and Jerusalem still under the British Mandate. It received harsh criticisms when debated in parliament. Even the Zionist Herbert Samuel, a former High Commissioner for Palestine, said:

> "The Commission seem to have gone to the Versailles Treaty and picked out all the most difficult and awkward provisions it contained. They have put a Saar, a Polish Corridor and half a dozen Danzigs and Memel into a country the size of Wales."[92]

A British Statement of Policy said that the government were much impressed by the advantages which partition offered to both the Arabs and the Jews. With regard to the Palestinian Arabs it said:

> "The Arabs would obtain their national independence, and thus be enabled to co-operate on an equal footing with the Arabs of the neighbouring countries in the cause of Arab unity and progress."[93]

Nevill Barbour, always a staunch supporter of justice for the Palestinians, commented:

> "When it was said that 'the Arabs' would obtain their national independence, what did this mean? … When a Palestinian Arab speaks of independence 'on equal footing with the Arabs of the neighbouring countries' he can but think of a country consisting of three-quarters of a million peasants cultivating their rich orange-groves, their bananas, their cereals, their maize, their sesame, their water-melons, their tobacco, their olives, and their apricots. He pictures to himself the busy sea-ports Jaffa and Haifa, and thinks of the latter's connexions with Iraq and the East. He thinks of the capital and its Holy Places, Muslim and Christian, to which Palestinian sentiment is so deeply attached. If he is a Muslim he thinks also of Ramleh and Acre and of the heroic achievements of Saladin. If he is a Christian he thinks of Bethlehem and Nazareth and of the Lake of Galilee. Above all

he thinks of the Palestinian soil of which his civilization is an essential and a congruous part.

Palestinian independence with any of these things removed could only be a maimed and halting thing. With almost all of them removed it would be no independence at all. Moreover, the 'independence' offered by the Commission was offered to only about one-half of 'the Arabs.' 'By means of partitioning' one-third were to be subordinated to Jewish domination immediately and for ever, while even in the new Mandatory Zone, or Corridor, there would appear to have been very good grounds for the Arab expectation that 'the fate of this area would be to grow increasingly Jewish and for its Arab population to decline.'"[94]

To an uncommitted observer, the idea of partition as a solution to the growing conflict in Palestine could seem quite attractive. It fits quite well with the idea of a Jewish National Home *in* Palestine, so that the Jews could live in one area and the Arabs in the other.

But to anyone who knew about the actual demographics of Palestine, it was of course unjustifiable nonsense. Even in the 1930s, as the British fostered waves of Jewish immigration to Palestine, the Palestinian Arabs were still in the majority. Furthermore, they lived all over Palestine. There wasn't a predominantly Arab area and a predominantly Jewish area which presented themselves for a map maker to draw neat boundaries. What there *was* was a predominantly Arab area all over Palestine, and pockets of Jews living in cities, villages, kibbutzim and on farms. Any attempt to carve out a contiguous area and hand it over for the exclusive use of Jews would inflict a major injustice on the hundreds of thousands of Palestinians in that area.

In fact, this particular partition scheme for Palestine never materialized after the Peel Commission's report. Yet another committee, the Woodhead Committee, was sent out to Palestine to assess the feasibility of the sort of division of the country that Peel (and Ben-Gurion) had suggested. It decided that the biggest obstacle to the plan was the fact that it required a large transfer of Arabs, which was unlikely to be carried out without objections from the Palestinians. Woodhead presented two other options for partition but these were rejected by the government because of insurmountable "political, administrative and financial difficulties".

Running out of ideas, the British government organised a round table conference of Zionists and Arabs, a proposal which was accepted by both parties as long as they didn't have to be in the same room together.

Malcom Macdonald, the current Colonial Secretary read a statement to each side which revealed that the government no longer felt it could bring peace to Palestine by force of arms and that it looked forward to establishing an independent democratic government to represent all the people of Palestine.

The Zionists were stunned. In spite of all their efforts, it seemed that the British had come to realise – rather belatedly – that the phrase 'Jewish National Home' should only be interpreted as a National Home and not a Jewish State. Their meeting did not last long and in a tense atmosphere the conference adjourned.

When the news of the government's volte face reached Palestine, with no more talk of partition and the hope of a fairer form of self-government, there were joyful demonstrations among Palestinians Arabs. Jews in Palestine marked their dissatisfaction with the news by planting a number of bombs among the celebrating Arabs, killing thirty-eight and wounding fourteen.

In spite of the government's reassurance, the Arab Revolt against the British was still continuing in Palestine and the government in London was alarmed enough at the events to issue another 'Statement of Policy' White Paper, which enlarged on the message it had given to the round table conference.

"Unauthorised statements have been made to the effect that the purpose in view is to create a wholly Jewish Palestine. Phrases have been used such as that 'Palestine is to become as Jewish as England is English'. His Majesty's Government regard any such expectation as impracticable and have no such aim in view. Nor have they at any time contemplated ... the disappearance or the subordination of the Arabic population, language or culture in Palestine. They would draw attention to the fact that the terms of the (Balfour) Declaration referred to do not contemplate that Palestine as a whole should be converted into a Jewish National Home, but that such a Home should be founded *in Palestine.* But this statement has not removed doubts, and His Majesty's Government therefore now declare unequivocally that it is not part of their policy that Palestine should become a Jewish State. They would indeed regard it as contrary to their obligations to the Arabs under the Mandate, as well as to the assurances which have been given to the Arab people in the past, that the Arab population of Palestine should be made the subjects of a Jewish State against their will."[95]

Well, there is no ambiguity there, and at the time, many Arabs believed it. Here's how one Palestinian writer reacted to this White Paper, issued in May 1939:

"Twenty-five years of anguish bordering on despair. Twenty-five years of fear, breeding hatred for a regime imposed on them without as much as by your leave. Twenty-five years of a continuous fierce struggle for their existence with the odds immeasurably weighted against them. Twenty-five years of discrimination in favour of the Jews by virtue of the Mandate. Twenty-five years of sporadic outbursts of temper at moments when the cup of endurance had been filled to overflowing. Twenty-five years of poverty, of misery and the sacrifice of life and at long last a straggling ray of light seemed to pierce the thick clouds around it and to re-kindle the dying embers of hope. That was the 17th day of May, 1939."[96]

Unfortunately, Mr Abcarius's sigh of relief was premature.

As we will see in a later chapter, the Partition idea was not dead, just sleeping, and another Partition scheme, devised in the UN, was to put the last nail in the coffin containing Palestinian hopes of independence.

Just as the half-baked Balfour Declaration slipped into official policy while the British government was trying to win the First World War, the discussions about possible solutions to the Palestine situation in the 1930s were overshadowed by the growing conflict that became the Second World War. And one factor above all others transformed the Zionist argument on the world stage to the huge detriment of the Palestinians.

As the Second World War unfolded, the Zionists increasingly promoted the idea that Palestine was the only 'safe haven' for Jews fleeing Nazi persecution and for those who survived the camps after the end of the war. They painted a picture that even after the defeat of Germany, Jews were unsafe anywhere but Palestine and that *all* Jews saw Palestine as their one hope of survival and freedom from persecution after the war. For the Zionists, the tragedy of the Holocaust and the plight of the survivors should therefore outweigh any sentimental attraction the Palestinian Arabs might have to their land.

The story of how the Zionists cynically manipulated that tragedy and betrayed many thousands of European Jews in the process is rarely told.

Chapter 6: "The things Jews are capable of doing…"

Some time during World War II, an Arab doctor in Jerusalem took up his pen and wrote a letter to the American president.

> "We all sympathize with the Jews and are shocked at the way Christian nations are persecuting them. But do you expect Moslems of Palestine … to be more Christian or more humanitarian than the followers of Christ: Germany, Italy, Poland, Romania, etc. etc.? Have we to suffer in order to make good what you Christians commit?"[97]

This doctor's letter reflected the Palestinians' frustration with the way in which the plight of Europe's Jews was used to raise support among Western nations for the Zionists' aims. Many uncommitted people might not be too impressed by Zionist arguments that *some* Jews had lived in *part* of Palestine thousands of years ago, but when stories emerged of the persecution and mass slaughter of Jews in Germany, and the plight of the 300,000 or so survivors, there was a ready audience for the Zionists' idea that these poor people would only be safe from future persecution in Palestine, and that Britain had a humanitarian duty to open the gates of Palestine, by abolishing restrictions on immigration or greatly increasing the number of visas they issued.

Using what we can call the 'safe haven' argument, Zionist organisations in the UK and America even argued that Palestinian Arabs should leave their own homes and communities to allow thousands of Displaced Persons (DPs), as they were called, to take refuge. One modern Israeli historian writes:

> "The onset of the Second World War and the Holocaust increased Zionist desperation to attain a safe haven in Palestine for Europe's persecuted Jews - and reinforced their readiness to adopt transfer [of Palestinian Arabs] as a way of instantaneously emptying the land so that it could absorb the prospective refugees from Europe."[98]

This implies that the only reason Zionists were desperate to bring Holocaust survivors to Palestine was to 'save' them in some way, but long-ignored evidence came to light at the beginning of this century showing that there were political and propaganda motives behind the Zionist push to get survivors to Palestine which sometimes led to coercion of survivors who didn't want to go, and some survivors being prevented from going because they were the 'wrong sort of Jew'.

This was not really surprising – Zionists had already shown in the 1920s and 30s that they were ready to say anything to achieve their aims. One Zionist even blamed Britain for the Holocaust:

> "The British had significant reluctance to allow a Jewish majority in the region. This led in later years to a policy of systematically reduced immigration quotas, and indirectly to the death of millions of Jewish refugees in Europe twenty some years later."[99]

Palestinian anger was now stoked by the global expectation, fomented by the Zionists, that the Palestinian Arabs were required to set their rights to one side to help solve a problem for which they were not to blame. As the Arab doctor's letter implied, everybody *but* the Palestinians had a duty to roll up their sleeves and help deal with the growing refugee crisis in Europe. The impact of 300,000 refugees on a western country like the USA or the UK, with populations numbered in tens of millions, would be far smaller than the impact on Palestine. Three hundred thousand people was more than 15% of the population of Palestine in 1945, but less than 0.3% of the US population. Surely the problem could be solved much more easily by the major powers combining to give sanctuary to the DPs?

To help understand the scale of the problem, President Truman sent a US judge, Earl G. Harrison, to Europe to talk to a range of organisations, visit the camps, and talk to survivors.

Harrison, as a typical example of someone who had power without responsibility, recommended opening the gates of

Palestine to all Jewish DPs, and he observed – wrongly –that "most Jews want to be evacuated to Palestine now, just as other national groups are being repatriated to their homes." This recommendation moved Truman to write a letter to British Prime Minister Clement Attlee, requesting that the British would provide 100,000 immigration certificates to Jewish refugees from Europe. Yozef Grodzinsky, in his book on the fate of the Jewish DPs, wrote:

> "This letter linked the Jewish holocaust to the establishment of a national home in Zion. It also turned survivors into potential immigrants to Palestine. Such suggestions were not new: Ben-Gurion ... had spoken of the 'Surviving Remnant' as a human reserve for the settlement of Palestine as early as 1943; others spoke in similar terms; even Weizmann, it had been rumored, had mentioned such ideas to Churchill."[100]

While it is true that the DPs were all *potential* immigrants to Palestine, the Zionists who flocked to Europe from Palestine to set about activating that immigration in the years after the War were dismayed to discover that many of the DPs did not actually want to go to Palestine at all.

A survey carried out in Dachau in 1945 showed that the vast majority of Jewish holocaust survivors who were questioned – 65% – wished to return home, to the countries in Europe from which they had fled or been taken. About 20% wanted to go to the United States, and only 15% wanted to immigrate to Palestine.[101]

If the Jewish organisations that set up offices in the DP camps had been concerned for the well-being of their fellow-Jews after their ghastly ordeals in Germany and Eastern Europe, they would presumably have helped the various Jewish DPs to achieve their personal aims, arranging transport back to their homes or lobbying the US and other European countries to take in the refugees, *in addition to* helping those who wanted to go to Palestine. In fact there was a range of Jewish organisations which did supply services in the camps to improve life for the refugees and start the task of planning the future they wanted for themselves after the end of the war.

But for one organisation, the Z.K., standing for 'Central Committee of Liberated Jews', the politics of Zionism were more important than the welfare of Holocaust survivors, and they set about trying to turn as many Jewish DPs as possible into citizens of Palestine, whether they liked it or not.

Yosef Grodzinsky is Professor of Psychology at Tel Aviv University and he has carried out detailed research into the activities of Zionists who descended on the Displaced Persons camps in Germany between 1945 and 1948. The cruel story he tells is difficult to believe in the light of widely propagated Zionist accounts of Palestine as a necessary 'safe haven' for all of Europe's Jews.

I hope to justify the use of the word 'cruel' by analysing two of the situations Professor Grodzinsky describes in his book *In the Shadow of the Holocaust.*

The first relates to the fate of the many children who survived the Holocaust and ended up, many as orphans, in the DP camps. What happened to some of them has echoes of a statement by David Ben-Gurion, quoted in his biography, when he said:

> "If I knew that it was possible to save all the children of Germany by transporting them to England, and only half by transferring them to the Land of Israel, I would choose the latter, for before us lies not only the numbers of these children but the historical reckoning of the people of Israel."[102]

No one denies that he said this, and Grodzinsky's research shows in detail how efforts by well-meaning Europeans to find loving homes for the hundreds of Jewish orphans in Europe were thwarted by Zionists who shared Ben-Gurion's view that Jewish children must be prevented from going anywhere but Palestine.

At the war's end, a group of British Jews persuaded the British government to grant entry permits for a thousand Jewish child survivors. With the agreement of the Home Office and the help of the RAF, the first three hundred landed in Carlisle and were bussed to a hostel on Lake Windermere, where they were looked after, taught English, given psychotherapy, and equipped with the skills they needed for the next stage of their lives.

"We had arrived in paradise", said Icek Alterman who had survived the concentration camps Auschwitz-Birkenau and Dachau.

About half of the children stayed in Britain, some of the rest went to the US, and some more, eventually, to Israel.

Other Jewish orphans had been adopted by Christian families and institutions elsewhere in Europe, but such rescue operations were seen by the Zionist 'rescuers' from Palestine as an affront to Zionism, and so members of the Jewish Agency tracked down Jewish children who had already been placed in families in order to take them away and gather them in orphanages, ready to be shipped out to Palestine when that became possible. Neither the children nor the foster parents were given any choice in the matter, and violence was sometimes used. One girl, Fanny Tirosh, remembered decades later the horrors of being snatched from a loving home by Zionist fanatics:

> "[Men] came in one day, armed, and threatened [our parents] saying that 'these are Jewish children and they must give us away, otherwise they would suffer'. They had no choice but hand us over, and we were put in a Jewish orphanage in Belgium [...] My sister told me, although I myself have no such memory, that we both refused to leave the house, and that to this very day, my screams still echo in her head. I did not want to go, for me it was a very cruel day when I was taken away from there."
> 103

Other rescue attempts were organised by well-meaning organisations, including sending children to Jewish schools in France and Switzerland, but this was still seen as threatening to the Zionists, as it ran counter to their insistence on bringing all surviving children to Palestine. Children were even forbidden from searching for their relatives in case this would lead to them staying in Europe.

At a meeting of the Central Committee of Liberated Jews in Bavaria, the following discussion took place, according to Professor Grodzinsky:

"'The few children we have,' reported Committee Member Puczyc at the opening of the session, 'need urgent, special help as winter approaches. We have appealed to the [Jewish Joint Committee] to do something for the children. Here in the camp we are about to send one group to England this week, and another to Switzerland soon. We have made a special effort to concentrate the children from all the camps in the St. Otilien Hospital [Munich], where they can be treated properly, and where they may prepare themselves for a new life.' Yet, unlike previous times, the idea of evacuation was not well received. 'Considering matters in Palestine,' said Engineer Leibovich, a representative from Munich. 'we must object to the evacuation of the children to England. England sends soldiers to Palestine. England must know that we are ready to give up on its hospitality until our problem is finally resolved.'"

This was the attitude of the Zionist groups which had travelled from Palestine to Europe to deal with the problem presented by the thousands of child holocaust survivors. Z.K. was not the only organisation trying to deal with the situation, but it was powerful enough for its views to predominate over other, more humanitarian, organisations. There were even children who appealed directly to Jewish aid organisations. Two of them, Gershon Pasanowsky, aged 14, and Bronia Katz, 15, wrote:

"For six years we were living in concentration camps and have until now not found our parents. They are probably not living anymore. We have decided to avail ourselves of England's offer to have orphans come to study there and to go to London immediately [...] We are looking forward to receiving your answer at the earliest possible moment, telling us what we have to do in order to proceed to London."[104]

Their appeal was ignored.

Meanwhile, all sorts of tricks and ruses were used to extricate orphans from orphanages, where their own wishes might be respected, and ship them off to Palestine. Jorge Garcia-Granados was a member of a UN committee exploring possible solutions to the Palestine issue. He described a conversation he had in one of the orphanages with a representative of the International Refugee Organisation, Miriam Woolpi, who told him:

> "One day this large group of children ... came up to me and asked if they could go on a picnic on the next day. I said, 'of course'. Life is so monotonous here that we are happy if they show sufficient interest to do something of that kind themselves. They went —" said Miss Woolpi —"and they did not return. We sent people out to look for them, but of course we could not find them. We knew what had happened only later."

A British newspaper correspondent asked:

> "Isn't it rather unusual to allow them to go off on picnics by themselves? I mean, aren't security precautions taken - doesn't a member of your staff go along?"

Miss Woolpi replied:

> "We sent along one of our staff. He did not return, either." [105]

In fact, Zionist proselytisers had taken the children away and put them on a ship, the *Exodus*, as it turned out. This American ship was built to carry 350 passengers but the Zionists crammed over 4500 refugees on board. It was claimed that its destination was Istanbul but in fact it was attempting an illegal entry to Palestine. But it was intercepted by the British navy and during the fighting which ensued two passengers died – one of them a boy from among the 'picnic children'. The refugees were eventually returned to DP camps in Germany, and in retaliation for the British actions against the ship, Jews in Palestine blew up a British police station, killing ten people and injuring 54.

When the French government agreed visas for 500 Jewish children, the news reached the Z.K. which issued a statement banning the transfer of the children:

"Liberated Jews have just one immigration option: Palestine. …
Either the children go to the place they need and have a right to
go to – Palestine, or they stay in the camps. We refuse to send
the five hundred children and fifty teachers to France."[106]

When Ben-Gurion heard of the efforts of some Jews to
organise the rescue of the children from the camps to France,
he said "The things Jews are capable of doing... incredible!"[107]

Professor Grodzinski sums up this episode, by quoting one
of the well-meaning Jewish organisers, Zorah Warhaftig:

"The steps Ben-Gurion and the Z.K. took … were successful: The
evacuation plan failed. This failure effectively blocked all the
paths out, except the one leading to Eretz Yisrael [Palestine]. In
view of the decisions of the DP Committees against the
temporary removal of children to other countries, we canceled
an additional plan to evacuate three thousand refugees and five
hundred children to Italy, a plan that had already been
negotiated with the authorities in Rome." [108]

The growing influence of Zionist envoys in the camps
upset many Jewish survivors who had no desire to go to
Palestine and tried to resist the pressure to do so. But they had
difficulty being heard. At one survivors' conference, a woman
called Miriam jumped on to the stage and spoke her mind: "It
must be demanded," she said, "that the gates of *all* countries,
not just Palestine, should be open to survivors."

This is what happened next:

"The crowd would not let her finish. People screamed, whistled,
jeered. Angry people in the audience waved their fists at her.
'Enough! Bring her down!' was the cry heard from all directions.
A young man, his fists tight, jumped to the stage and pounced
at her. She was not scared. She was boiling with fury, why
wouldn't they let her speak? But she was dragged down the
steps. As she tried to force her way through the crowd, she felt
that one more moment they would have lynched her."[109]

In the DP camps that the UN committee visited, the
members were given almost identical answers when they
asked the DPs they met where they would like to go:

"No matter to whom we spoke, in whatever language – German, Russian, Polish, Rumanian, Hungarian, Yiddish - the desire was one: to go to Palestine and only to Palestine."

An American officer, General Clay, was asked by the Committee:

"'Have you heard of any organisations behind the movement for immigration to Palestine?'

General Clay looked soberly at the table before him. 'I have heard many suggestions that such was the case, but it has never been proved,' he said. 'There is, of course, an indoctrination of the people by their own leaders that they must go to Palestine.'"[110]

A comment by a visitor to the camps as part of a UN inquiry shows how successful the Zionist pressure had been on the DPs to say they wanted to go to Palestine:

"Mr. Garcia-Granados ... went on to say that among the Jews questioned in German and Austrian camps by the ... Special Committee there had not been one who had not expressed his determination to get to Palestine. That was a psychological fact." [111]

By this stage, two years after the end of the War, the Z.K. and others had had plenty of time to indoctrinate the survivors. And indoctrination was what they needed if the maximum number was to assert that they wanted to go to Palestine, as Grodzinski describes:

"'We must not think that thousands upon thousands will come knocking at the country's gates once they open,' said Ze'ev Schind (alias Danny), a senior Mossad commander. A practical man, he made a concrete suggestion: 'The Zionist movement must understand that it has to be first on the market. All the political parties in Diaspora will not have the strength needed to lift the Jews to acts of Zionism, and thus our own envoys must move and work together with the Allied armies.'"[112]

From 1947 it was clear that the situation in Palestine was moving towards some kind of armed confrontation if the Jews were to take over the state from the Palestinian Arabs. But in order to carry out hostilities, the *Yishuv* would need many more able-bodied people to train in guerrilla tactics. In the camps in Europe, among the population that ranged in age from children to old people, there would be a pool of young men who could be conscripted by the Zionist organisations in the camps, and shipped, often illegally, to Palestine. Extracting fighters from the DPs and shipping them to Palestine was a new priority which overrode the needs of other, less able, Jewish refugees.

Early in 1947, a French group of Jews sent a boat with more than 800 child survivors to Palestine, but they received a telegram from the Zionist authorities in Palestine saying:

> "You may not send children till further notice. ... All the institutions are angry about the composition of the shipments. The agent [supreme commander] has made a categorical demand to bring [...through illegal immigration...] only for the draft. The agent demands to halt the immigration of even *Exodus* people until May, and to prefer trained personnel for the war effort." [113]

In the camps, the Zionist emissaries set about finding refugees with the right characteristics to be conscripted into the Jewish militias in Palestine. At a congress of refugee organisations in Germany, a leader of the largest paramilitary organisation in Palestine, General Nahum Shadmi, addressed the meeting:

> "He presented a brief political and military analysis of the situation, which led to the conclusion that 'therefore, every young man and woman, aged 18-35, must join the Haganah whose role is to protect us from the Arabs, perhaps even from the British army. Everyone must be in the Haganah – there are no excuses [...] All those capable, must mobilize and come to Eretz Israel and join the army.'" [114]

Another delegate supported Shadmi's speech and proposed that:

"Jews who do not fulfill their duty and register, will be declared as deserters."[115]

Professor Grodzinsky points out that:

"It is difficult to find justification to the conscription of non-citizens, who live outside the territory of the coercive government, who had never set foot there, do not speak the local language, and for the most part have no interest in going there."[116]

But the conscription (*Giyus* in Yiddish) was imposed on all suitable people in the camps, in spite of the fact that they had European citizenships which were not under the control of the Jewish authorities in Palestine and even if they had no desire to take up arms in a faraway Middle Eastern country. One reporter wrote in a Jewish magazine in New York:

"Most Jewish refugees who had been through the hell of the ghetto, slavery and death camps under the Nazis, Soviet forced-labor camps, and other disasters, yearn for some quiet place. Regardless of their views on current events in Palestine, they feel physically drained, and have no desire to go into the fire again. They rightfully ask – even the Zionists among them – why do we, having been so pained and tortured, need to go back into the fire?" [117]

Those survivors who refused to have anything to do with the Zionist draft could be sanctioned in a variety of ways. According to the Z.K. Congress:

"The Congress is imposing a *Giyus* registration duty on all men and women aged 17 to 35, who must make themselves available for the service of the people; The Congress decided that all *Giyus* dodgers who do not fulfill their duty will be removed from the social and political life and will be denied entry to all offices."[118]

In the DP camps, employees were fired, residents were evicted from their apartments, others were fined, or denied the supplementary food that was being distributed to all camp Jews; others were simply subjected to violence.

Near Ulm, for example, "a father of *Giyus* evader Wecker was beaten up, as was the father of one who did not register; in another case an old father, Richter Aizik, was beaten because his son Moshe Richter did not register for the *Giyus*."[119]

Grodzinsky quotes just two of the many official orders, punishing holocaust survivors who refused to go to Palestine and fight.

"To the Jewish Committee In Camp Rochelle We hereby inform you of the decision of the Committee for the Service of the People, to the effect that the following people cannot be employed in their present work places: 1. Goldstein Maniek (shops) 2. Gorland Moshé (tailor shop) 3. Zilber Chayim (tailor shop) 4. Armeiner Hans (director of sports club) 5. Hor Moshé (secretary of the League) We demand that you carry out these instructions immediately. (-) Commission for the Service of the People."[120]

"Commission for the Service of the People in Camp Rochelle: Please note that when handing out the Joint rations to tailors and knitters for the months March-April, you should not hand out the rations for the second half of April to persons who had been fired from their jobs on the 15.4 by the *Giyus* Commission. Commission for the Service of the People."[121]

In spite of the efforts of the Zionist 'press-gangs' the majority of Jewish survivors did not go to Palestine. Although, once Israel was established it was easier for them to go there than to any other country, only 40% or so ended up as Israeli citizens. Many – including many of the DP leaders – ended up in the United States, after moves in Congress to prevent the admission of DPs were finally overturned.

I have gone into these episodes at some length because they are so different from the way we might have expected Jews to behave if they were genuinely concerned about the dreadful plight of DPs in Europe. And although it might seem irrelevant to the theme of this book – the series of hammer blows to Palestinian freedom dealt by the advocates of Zionism over thirty years – it provides one more example of the lies that were told to, and about, the Palestinians by

Zionists, in their efforts, eventually successful, to take Palestine from the Palestinians. For during the Second World War, the Palestinians were told that increased immigration of Jews to Palestine was essential for humanitarian reasons, to save the thousands of Holocaust survivors whose only hope was to live their lives in Palestine. They – and most people in the West – never discovered how the hopes, and sometimes lives, of Holocaust survivors were sacrificed to benefit the most dogmatic and uncompromising form of Zionism.

The effect on the rest of the world of the false linking of "the Jewish holocaust to the establishment of a national home in Zion" as Grodzinsky put it, harmed Palestinians in another way. It turned uncommitted people against their case for a Palestinian state of all its inhabitants, making the Palestinians seem merciless and lacking in compassion in the face of Zionist arguments that mass Jewish immigration was the only way to save Holocaust survivors.

Chapter 7: Britain gives up

When Britain admitted to itself and then to the world in 1939 that reconciling the twin requirements of the Mandate was unachievable, the nine years that followed could have progressed along two different paths. One of those paths culminated in five Arab armies moving up to the partition line separating the new Jewish state from Arab areas, to prevent or stop the continuing Jewish attacks, destruction, and massacres in Arab towns and villages, and the expulsion of 750,000 Palestinians. But what was the other path?

I ask this to assess whether, in spite of the accumulation of insults, injustices and lies the Palestinians had been subjected to over the previous twenty years, some moderation of Zionist behaviour might have achieved a compromise by which both sides achieved some, if not all, of what they wanted, and by which 75 years of tragic loss of life and suffering might have been avoided.

There were certainly Jews who argued for another path – Jews not Zionists – as Edward Said wrote in an article in the *New York Times* in 1999:

> "During the interwar period, a small but important group of Jewish thinkers (Judah Magnes, [Martin] Buber, [Hannah] Arendt and others) argued and agitated for a binational state. The logic of Zionism naturally overwhelmed their efforts, but the ... essence of their vision is coexistence and sharing in ways that require an innovative, daring and theoretical willingness to get beyond the arid stalemate of assertion and rejection. Once the initial acknowledgment of the other as an equal is made, I believe the way forward becomes not only possible but also attractive."[122]

Judah Magnes was a rabbi who saw only too clearly how the Zionists' dogmatism and refusal to compromise would make impossible a peaceful resolution of the conflict. He became Chancellor of the Hebrew University and in 1929 he made a speech there in which he said:

"If we cannot find ways of peace and understanding, if the only way of establishing the Jewish National Home is upon the bayonets of some Empire, our whole enterprise is not worthwhile, and it is better that the Eternal People that has outlived many a mighty empire should possess its soul in patience... It is one of the great civilizing tasks before the Jewish people to enter the promised land, not in the Joshua way, but bringing peace and culture, hard work and sacrifice and love, and a determination to do nothing that cannot be justified before the conscience of the world."[123]

Judah Magnes, one of the few Jewish leaders in Palestine who saw the injustice of the Zionist claims to the country.

Bearing in mind what we have seen so far of the single-minded and sometimes vicious pursuit of a Jewish state by Weizmann and his supporters, we can imagine how little these peace-seeking words of Magnes might have been appreciated by the Zionists and their British politician friends. And yet Magnes, who lived in Palestine among Palestinian Arabs, foresaw exactly the problems that would face Jews and Arabs over the next two decades. In an article in the *New York Times* in 1937, he wrote:

"With the permission of the Arabs we will be able to receive hundreds of thousands of persecuted Jews in Arab lands [...] Without the permission of the Arabs even the four hundred thousand [Jews] that now are in Palestine will remain in danger, in spite of the temporary protection of British bayonets."[124]

But Magnes found few takers among the Zionists for his messages of peace. When the Peel Commission published its partition plan, Magnes addressed a meeting and said:

"What is the Jewish state that is being offered? It is a Jewish State which, in my opinion, will lead to war, to war with the Arabs. (Laughter.) Perhaps the man who laughed has not been through what happened last year [referring to the Arab Revolt]. I was. My sons were. The sons and daughters of my friends were. I see some of my comrades from Palestine here who were. It is not a laughing matter for them … Why will it lead to war? In the first place because the Jewish state as it is offered to us contains lands about three quarters of which are in the hands of Arabs…"[125]

Of course, for the Zionists, a partition of Palestine which left hundreds of thousands of Arabs in a Jewish state was only a temporary problem. There was plenty of evidence since 1917 that the expulsion of Palestinians from their own land was seen as perfectly acceptable by Zionists. In Jabotinsky's words, they could just be 'broomed' out of the Jewish state.

When Chaim Weizmann met the Russian ambassador, Ivan Maiskii, in London in 1941 to discuss possible orange exports to Russia, the conversation turned to the subject of population transfer as a means of creating space for more Jews in Palestine. Benny Morris the Israeli historian, quotes from Maiskii's report of the conversation:

"Weizmann, according to Maiskii, had proposed 'to move a million Arabs to Iraq, and to settle four or five million Jews from Poland and other countries on the land where these Arabs were.' The Soviet ambassador had expressed surprise regarding Weizmann's expectation of settling four or five million Jews on lands inhabited by only one million Arabs. Weizmann replied, according to Maiskii: 'Oh, don't worry …The Arab is often called the son of the desert. It would be truer to call him the father of the desert. His laziness and primitivism turn a flourishing garden into a desert. Give me the land occupied by one million Arabs, and I will easily settle five times that number of Jews on it." [126]

(In spite of twenty years encountering Palestine and Palestinians, Weizmann still believed – or pretended to believe – that all Palestinians were primitive bedouins or fellahin.)

While there was not unanimity among the Palestinian Arabs about a lot of things, there had always been agreement among all Palestinians about the fact that a Jewish state in Palestine and the political rights of the indigenous Palestinian population were incompatible. The Mufti, Haj Amin, appointed by the British as leader of a group of senior Arabs, set his face against any compromise, and resisted the efforts of his more pro-British fellow committee members to get him to accept the partition recommendations of the Peel Commission. But for some more moderate Palestinian leaders, a Palestinian state with Jewish citizens – the bi-national state Edward Said promoted – would have been acceptable to the Palestinian Arabs, if it had ever been seriously offered by the British and accepted by the Jews.

In Britain, there were several factors which drove the government finally to wash its hands of the whole issue. There was its preoccupation with another World War, the rejections by Arabs and Jews of every proffered 'solution', growing anti-British violence mainly by Jewish groups, including newly ascendant Jewish terrorist organisations, and constant wrangling over Jewish immigration, fuelled by the Zionist insistence on extra quotas for persecuted Jews from Europe. But Britain's attempts to be a broker between Arabs and Jews were thwarted by pressure exerted by the American government on Britain at the behest of strong Zionist representations from America's Jewish community.

Ernest Bevin, the British Foreign Minister, was angered beyond measure by the American interference in last-gasp British attempts to obtain a solution. In a speech in parliament he gave vent to his frustration:

"I did reach a stage in meeting the Jews separately, in which I advanced the idea of an interim arrangement, leading ultimately to self-government. I indicated that I did not mind whether this interim arrangement was for five years, or 10 years, or three years, or whatever it was. I said to them, 'If you will work together for three, five, or 20 years, it might well be that you will not want to separate. Let us try to make up the difference.' At that stage things looked more hopeful. There was a feeling—I do not think I overestimated it—when they left me in the Foreign Office that day, that I had the right approach at last. But what happened? Next day … my right honourable friend the Prime Minister telephoned me at midnight, and told me that the President of the United States was going to issue another statement on the 100,000 [immigrants]. I think the country and the world ought to know about this.

I went next morning to the Secretary of State, Mr. Byrnes, and told him how far I had got the day before. I believed we were on the road, if only they would leave us alone. … I hope I am not saying anything to cause bad feeling with the United States, but I feel so intensely about this. A vexed problem like this, with a thousand years of religious differences, has to be handled with the greatest detail and care. No one knows that more than I do. I have seen these tense religious struggles in parts of this country, in Ireland, and elsewhere. I know what it involves. It can lead to civil war before you know where you are. However, the statement was issued. I was dealing with Jewish representatives at the time, and I had to call it off because the whole thing was spoilt."[127]

There was already no love lost between Bevin and the US administration. The year before, at the Labour Party conference he had said that the United States wished to see 100,000 Jews in Palestine because they "did not want too many Jews in New York".[128] Although this remark appalled British diplomats, the US Congress *had* resisted efforts by some Jewish relief agencies to allow Holocaust survivors to emigrate to the United States.

President Truman himself, in private, was no lover of the Jews, but the pressure on him from leading American Jews and Jewish organisations was too great to resist. Questioned about this by a group of visitors he said:

"I am sorry gentlemen, but I have to answer to hundreds of thousands who are anxious for the success of Zionism. I do not have hundreds of thousands of Arabs among my constituents."[129]

His private diary entries show his true feelings:

"The Jews have no sense of proportion nor do they have any judgement on world affairs. [They] are very, very selfish. They care not how many Estonians, Latvians, Finns, Poles, Yugoslavs or Greeks get murdered or mistreated as D[isplaced] P[ersons] as long as the Jews get special treatment. Yet when they have power, physical, financial or political, neither Hitler nor Stalin has anything on them for cruelty or mistreatment to the underdog. Put an underdog on top and it makes no difference whether his name is Russian, Jewish, Negro, Management, Labor, Mormon, Baptist he goes haywire. I've found very, very few who remember their past condition when prosperity comes."[130]

(Read in the light of today's treatment of Palestinians by Israel, this diary entry has a prophetic character.)

The British government had reached the end of the road. Between 1946 and 1947 Britain had tried to collaborate with America in the search for a solution, starting with a joint Anglo-American Committee of Inquiry in 1946. This argued for a single unitary state to include both Arabs and Jews, the continuation of Jewish immigration and land purchases, and the disarming of the Jewish underground armies in Palestine. True to Zionist form, when questioned about Jewish terror groups by the Committee, Ben-Gurion lied and said that he had no connection with them.

No one liked the Committee's plan and so two politicians, Henry Grady for the US and Herbert Morrison for the UK, came up with a new plan which proposed to divide Palestine into four areas – an Arab province, a Jewish province, a district of Jerusalem, and the Negev desert to be administered by the British Mandate. This plan proved equally unworkable.

When Bevin then proposed to prolong the Mandate for another five years, admitting a further 100,000 Jews, and setting up a joint Arab-Jewish advisory council, both Arabs and Jews rejected it. The decision about what to do next was announced by Bevin in Parliament on February 17th, 1947:

> "We have ... reached the conclusion that the only course now open to us is to submit the problem to the judgment of the United Nations. We intend to place before them an historical account of the way in which His Majesty's Government have discharged their trust in Palestine over the last 25 years. We shall explain that the Mandate has proved to be unworkable in practice, and that the obligations undertaken to the two communities in Palestine have been shown to be irreconcilable." [131]

It was a unilateral decision but Britain could argue that since the League of Nations – which had granted the Mandate to Britain – no longer existed having been replaced by the UN, it was entitled to do this.

It is worth taking a step back at this stage to analyse what Palestinians were thinking as they watched two great world powers try to decide their fate. The Palestinian Arabs were still the majority population of Palestine and their claims of independence were no weaker than they had been when Britain took control. In fact, the Peel Commission's report and a British government 'Statement of Policy' White Paper showed a degree of frustration with the pressure for Palestine to become a Jewish state, and an acceptance that the Arabs deserved some form of independence.

But having suffered years of Zionist calumnies, denials of justice, uncontrolled Jewish immigration, and blatant bias against them by the *Yishuv*, the Palestinians were not terribly impressed by the way their fate was being tossed around by statesmen who came out for a few days to Palestine, stayed in nice hotels, were bombarded with Zionist propaganda, glimpsed a few picturesque Arab villages, and went home. It is true to say that there had come a point where Palestinian Arabs had refused to talk to yet another committee, although it's worth bearing in mind that the British had exiled many senior leaders in the Arab community so it was difficult for them to make their arguments.

But no one can argue that the Arab case was not heard during the years that Britain and others wrestled with the problem. Palestinians were *heard* on many occasions but, it seemed to the Palestinians, never listened to. The last occasion on which a Palestinian Arab leader summarized the Palestinian case was at the London conference in early 1947, at the time it was becoming clear that Britain was going to wash its hands of Palestine. Jamal El-Husseini, vice-chairman of the Arab Higher Committee, addressed the conference. He said the Palestine Arab case was simple and self-evident:

"It was that of a people who desired to remain in undisturbed possession of their country, and to safeguard their national existence in freedom. This natural right happily coincided with the high principle of self-determination and of a series of promises and pledges which were given to the Arabs by the Government of Great Britain, who occupied Palestine after having declared to the world that they entered the Holy Land as allies and deliverers of its people and not as conquerors.

During the last 25 years, however, Palestine had been denied the right to self-government, in violation of those rights and pledges as well as the covenant of the League of Nations. An autocratic administration was set up with the primary aim of assisting the Jews in their invasion of Palestine. The Balfour Declaration on which this policy was based was a vague and one-sided encouragement made by Great Britain to alien Jews in the absence and complete ignorance of the Arab owners of the country.

Since 1918 the Jewish elements in Palestine had increased by enforced migration from 7 per cent to 33 per cent of the entire population ... During this period Jewish political claims had inflated from a modest spiritual home to the establishment of a Jewish state which they sought to enforce by the present campaign of terrorism. This had driven the Arabs to the point of exasperation, for they beheld that all the apprehensions they had expressed 25 years ago were being rapidly fulfilled.

Certain quarters had proposed that justice might be done if the country were partitioned between Arabs and Jews. The Arabs believed that such a proposal was an easy pretext for evading the difficulties of a problem that had been created by a gross injustice. The creation of an alien Jewish state in Palestine would mean a running sore that would undoubtedly become a permanent source of trouble in the Middle East, and would mean the destruction of Arab continuity and territorial sovereignty."[132]

Concise, unpolemical, factual and, as it turns out, prophetic.

From the day Britain abandoned Palestine to the mercies of the United Nations, some kind of partition of the land between Jews and Arabs – a 'running sore' to the Palestinians Arabs – was the front runner, under pressure from Zionism which refused to accept any shared role in the state in which they were still a minority.

The United Nations set up one more committee, called the United Nations Special Committee on Palestine, UNSCOP. The task of its eleven members, delegates from various UN member nations, was to "make recommendations … concerning the future government of Palestine".

A memoir by one of the members of UNSCOP does not inspire confidence in the objectivity or indeed the intelligence that was applied to the task. Although he was just one of the members, by his own account Jorge Garcia-Granados played a leading role in shaping the Committee's majority recommendation for partition. Granados was the Guatemalan delegate to the UN, a man who had had little or no contact with the Palestine issue before. Indeed, the UN itself had only been in existence for two years and the organisation was still trying to create a role for itself in world governance.

If it was not an overused joke, I would describe Granados' memoir, called *The Birth of Israel*, as 'Gullible's Travels'. He lacks the kind of questioning spirit someone would display who saw the seriousness of the task ahead and realised his own inadequacies:

> "I could not know that this request [to join UNSCOP] would change the course of my life in the following year and would plunge me deep into a problem which then had little or no meaning for me. Within a few months I was no longer to be my country's Ambassador to Washington but once more embroiled, as I had been so often before, in a people's fight for freedom. It was no special knowledge on my part that led my colleagues to think of me as a member of the investigating committee. I knew very little about Palestine. But they were sure that once I was convinced where justice lay, I would fight for it with all the energy at my command."[133]

From Granados' statement about becoming 'embroiled…in a people's fight for freedom' it seems fairly clear where Granados was 'convinced where justice lay' from the beginning. I suspect it was not the Arabs' fight for freedom he got embroiled in. In quoting from an American Jewish leader, Abba Silver, Granados swallows whole an account of the Balfour Declaration which has almost as many errors in it as the number of words:

> "A generation ago the international community of the world, of which the United Nations today is the political and spiritual heir, decreed that the Jewish people shall be given the right long denied and the opportunity to reconstitute their national home in Palestine. That national home is still in the making. It has not yet been fully established. No international community has cancelled, or even questioned, that right."[134]

The UNSCOP membership consisted of the delegates from Australia, Canada, Czechoslovakia, Guatemala, India, Iran, Netherlands, Peru, Sweden, Uruguay and Yugoslavia. They arrived in Palestine in June, 1947, and started touring the country and talking to as many people who would agree to talk to them. The overwhelming number of encounters was with Zionists and other Jews. The Arab Higher Committee, or the members of it who were not in exile, boycotted the Committee. They had learnt enough about UNSCOP to believe that it was pro-Zionist. Of course, being exposed overwhelmingly to the Zionist case and hearing much less about the Palestinian Arabs' case might be expected to bias their views, were it not for the fact that decades of official reports, including a three-volume work prepared by the British government for the Anglo-American Committee, would reveal a reasoned and eloquent account of the basis of the Arab claim for Palestine. In any case, twenty years of attempts by the Arabs to get justice or even merely comprehension of their arguments from government officials or visiting committees had failed to move the pointer on the dial away from Zionism and towards justice, and the Palestinians were weary of yet more polite conversations over cups of coffee with people from faraway places who knew little of Palestine.

Like so many first-time visitors to Palestine, Garcia-Granados seems to have been unable to look beneath the surface of what he saw:

"Side by side with the 20th century, we saw vestiges of the 15th. Arab water carriers, bent almost double under huge pigskins filled with water, trudged along the sidewalk, clapping together two tin cups to call attention to their wares; and now and then a donkey ambled along the road followed by an Arab switching him with a stick, while automobiles sounding their horns impatiently queued up behind them. "[135] ...

"To us, coming from the new city [Tel Aviv], the contrast was striking; it was as if we had leaped across the centuries into the Middle Ages. I felt the weight of time as I moved through the incredibly narrow up-hill, down-hill streets, some of them more properly passageways than streets, where merchants, clad in their native garments, sold all kinds of goods – clothes, silverware, sandals, meats, candy black with the flies that covered everything. We pushed our way forward, obliged now and then to move aside to make room for a water carrier riding on a small donkey, his bare feet dangling almost to the filthy cobblestoned pavement. Camels plodded down the narrow alleys, their heads almost touching the balconies of ancient stone houses picturesquely built on different levels." [136]

Garcia-Granados seemed to think that people who have to cope with flies and dirt, ride on donkeys, and haven't got access to the sort of massive investment that built Tel Aviv, don't deserve independence. In fact, he seems to have been a Zionist from the beginning. He didn't even seem troubled by the fact of Jewish terrorism. After describing a few of the many Jewish terrorist actions Palestine was suffering at the time, Granados says:

"No matter how we viewed such activities, the terrorists were inhabitants of the country, playing a definite role in the drama, and were entitled to express their views to UNSCOP." [137]

Granados' benign attitude to Jewish terrorists, whom he saw as 'patriots', comes out in his remark to one of his co-committee members:

"Many of these Jewish underground fighters were trained by the British themselves to sabotage industries, to wreck railroads, to dynamite buildings, to kill collaborationists and spies, and to commit all these acts which are now labelled terrorism. We call it terror now. Then we called it patriotism." [138]

He complained about vexations inflicted by British soldiers and police upon his Jewish chauffeur but if he had been able to read Secret Service files at the time he would have discovered that his 'Jewish chauffeur' was almost certainly a Zionist spy, planted to monitor the informal conversations of the UNSCOP members.

The Arabs might have expected some weight to be given by UNSCOP to the centuries during which they and their ancestors lived in the ancient towns and villages of Palestine, but Garcia-Granados manages to give an account of the history of Palestine and the events since the end of the First World War without mentioning any of its inhabitants, or considering their rights:

"The final conclusion of my study was clear: a country possessing sovereign rights (Turkey) over a territory (Palestine) had ceded them unconditionally to a group of nations (the

European Allies). These nations, in accord with traditional international usages, were entitled to pass upon the destinies of that land, to make provision for any kind of immigration into it, and to establish the form of government they saw fit. Consequently the Allies had assigned Palestine to Great Britain (the Mandatory) and had charged her to bring about a specific objective (the constitution of a Jewish National Home). The legal case of the Jews, it seemed to me, was far stronger than that of the Arabs." [139]

Garcia-Granados appears to have had no time for the idea that the people who lived in a discrete territory and whose families had lived there for generations should have any say in their own government. He also appears to have been unaware of the double obligation of the Mandate, to Jews and Arabs, something that the British themselves came to realise – rather belatedly – presented some difficulties, but as far as Garcia-Granados was concerned this presented no problem at all, since he had been sucked firmly into the Zionist camp.

Once the Committee had returned to New York, they had to produce some recommendations. Garcia-Granados – I suspect from the beginning – had favoured partition. This was the only way an exclusively Jewish state could be achieved in Palestine. But like everyone else who had wrestled with the issue, UNSCOP discovered that there was no rational way to separate Jewish areas from Arab areas. It was hardly surprising. For hundreds of years Palestinian Arabs had lived all over Palestine, from the hills of Judea to the coastal plain. They and their conquerors had built cities like Jaffa and Acre and Haifa and Safad and Jerusalem and Nablus, the places Garcia-Granados and his committee colleagues might have seen as 'mediaeval', but they held hundreds of thousands of Palestinians, living in houses and buying from shops and worshipping in mosques and churches, and learning in schools.

Almost overnight, in chronological terms, Jews had started arriving and, as Arthur Koestler noted, they did not learn from the Arabs to build houses which would fit the climate and landscape but merely transplanted their previous way of life. Far from founding the basis of a Jewish state, they interspersed their communities among the much older and far more numerous Arab population.

As others had discovered before them, when the UNSCOP members sat down to devise a partition plan, every idea they had was thwarted by facts on the ground. It was like spending a few weeks in an English county and then trying to partition it into two areas, one for people earning more than £50,000 p.a., say, and the other for people earning less. You would soon discover that, apart from pockets of rather expensive housing, any area you discovered with a conglomeration of high incomes would nevertheless contain numerous sites with low incomes. It may seem a fanciful analogy, but you would probably get a similar result if dividing up Palestine. Any area with the minority group – richer or Jewish – would contain many of the majority – poorer or Arab, whereas you could more easily carve out an area for the majority that was populated by far fewer of the minority.

Reading Garcia-Granados' account of how he and the other members of the committee went about the task makes it sound more like an elaborate board game than a serious task that would end up affecting the lives of millions. Here are a few extracts, showing a group of people giving away someone else's country with as much care or indeed logic as if they were swapping characters in a card game of *Happy Families*:

"Garcia Salazar was ready to give the Jews the whole of Galilee, but not the Negev. ... Sandstrom at the beginning had more or less shared this plan, then later appeared somewhat dubious about Western Galilee ... The technical difficulties were these. First, Galilee had a large Arab population and a small Jewish one; and was the only really fertile land in Palestine. ... if we gave Western Galilee to the Arabs and the Western Negev to the Jews, both lands would be separated from their states and be practically isolated.

As I studied this I began to evolve a new plan. I spoke first to Garcia Salazar, and offered to drop my opposition to a free city of Jerusalem if he would support my proposal to extend the

Jewish State's coastal strip to the Lebanese border. … I also devised two narrow international corridors … I think Rand will agree to any solution leading to agreement among us. … I shall speak to Fabregat; and I don't think Lisicky would wish to break such unanimity. …I spoke to them; I entreated them, and I think I came to convince them of the urgent necessity of accepting an arrangement based upon my plan. Mohn proposed that we let the Arabs have Western Galilee but assign to the Jews most of the Negev. When we had visited it we realized how much they could do with that wasteland, how eager they were to develop it, and how little the Arabs could do, or wished to do, with it."[140]

Note how they were 'giving' territory to people who had no legitimate claim to it and 'letting people have' towns and villages they had possessed for generations. But it sounds as if the Commission enjoyed themselves:

"We had finished our work. It was a great moment. A sincere desire to reach a solution, a largeness of vision which enabled even the most bitterly insistent to compromise, had enabled us to complete a report of which I felt all of us could be justly proud."[141]

In a UN session in October, Granados gave some interesting insights into his thinking on the topic, as summarised in the official report. First off, he gave short shrift to the idea that any inhabitant of a country would imagine they were entitled to have some say in their own fate.

"In the light of the Treaty of Lausanne and international practice after the two world wars, it was clear that however inconceivable it might appear to some people, the inhabitants of any particular region had no say in international conferences at which their fate was decided. The Arab argument regarding the self-determination of peoples constituted an ideal, but not an axiom of international law."[142]

A summary of his views suggests that he favoured a much better criterion for deciding who should govern Palestine than consulting the inhabitants, with strong echoes of Harry

Sacher's 'qualitative democracy' put forward thirty years beforehand.

> "Regarding the ... argument put forward by the Arabs, that of numerical superiority, Mr. Garcia Granados' view was that what characterized a nation was its culture and not the number of inhabitants. In twenty-five years, the Jewish people had left upon Palestine the indelible mark of an outstanding culture, which characterized the country even more than the Arab culture: Palestine was no more Arab than certain Spanish countries of Latin America were Indian." [143]

Granados' last remark reflects his spirit of patronising colonialism that was already dying out in Europe after the Second World War but was still obviously alive and kicking in Central and South America, because it reflected the contempt he had for the rights of the indigenous peoples of his own country, the 'Indians'. Granados would not even accept the 'Arabness' of the Palestinians, giving an extraordinary reason for this view:

> "The Holy Places and all the monuments of the two religions bore witness to the fact that Palestine was not Arab..." [144]

What happened next, the vote on the UNSCOP partition plan in the UN General Assembly, was accompanied by one of the most disgraceful campaigns waged by the Zionists and their American allies in the whole history of the loss of Palestine.

Chapter 8: No pressure, then

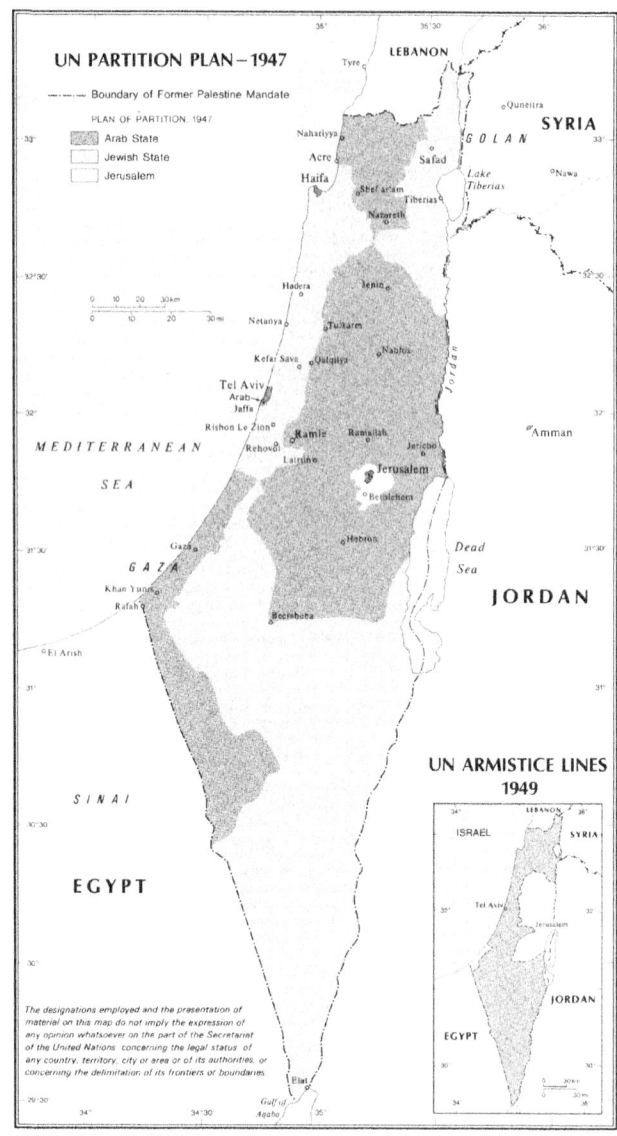

MAP NO. 3067 Rev. 1   UNITED NATIONS
APRIL 1983

98

The partition plan drawn up by UNSCOP was an attempt to divide the whole of Palestine – the territory between the Jordan river and the Mediterranean – into a Jewish state and an Arab state. This might have been possible if the two populations lived in different areas. But as the UNSCOP members found when they attempted the task, that was not how Palestine demography worked. The Arabs were all over the country, not surprisingly since they had lived there for centuries; the Jews, only a third of the population even after legal and illegal immigration, were in more discrete pockets, in areas which before they came along had been wholly Arab.

The result, as Palestinian historian Walid Khalidi wrote, was that

"75% cent of the total area of Palestine [was allocated] to the Jews at a time when their land ownership constituted 7.0 per cent of this area - an increase of more than 1000 per cent at Arab expense. The number of Jewish settlements to come under Arab rule was *ten* with a total of some 2000 inhabitants or a quarter of one per cent of the total Jewish population of the country. The number of Arab towns and villages to come under Jewish rule would be about 450, with a total of about 700,000 inhabitants, or 58 per cent of the total Arab population of the country. The Arabs would lose all their richest lands including all their citrus groves, which latter produced their most lucrative export crop. They would lose all control of the vital head-waters of the River Jordan, and all contact with the sea except for a tiny corridor leading to the largest Arab city of Jaffa, which from a bustling prosperous city would become a waif dependent on Jewish mercy."[145]

The Zionists had argued strongly that the Negev, a desert area in the south of Palestine, should be part of their new state. Khalidi points out that it was argued that the Jews should have this area because they can 'make the desert bloom.' By 1946, there were only four Jewish settlements in the Negev, with a population of 475. In the same area there were 100,000 Arabs, members of bedouin tribes which had been in the Negev for generations. The area cultivated by the Jewish settlements was a hundredth of the area cultivated by the bedouin. Khalidi goes on to demolish the 'blooming' cliché:

> "Plainly, and despite all the talk, the Jews simply did not make the desert bloom, nor were they indeed very interested in doing so. And if there was any blooming in the desert, this was the work of the wretchedly poor bedouins. Perhaps more to the point is that the area put by the bedouins under cultivation in the Negev was three times the total area cultivated by the entire Jewish community in Palestine, after more than sixty years of loudly trumpeted pioneering". [146]

It hardly needs to be said that the Arab states, on behalf of the Palestinians – who had no voice in the UN – objected strongly to UNSCOP's recommendation for the partition of Palestine. But they had hopes that they could achieve enough votes from nations which saw the injustice of the plan to prevent Resolution 181, as it was named, being passed.

The partition plan was debated by the UN General Assembly in late November, 1947, after several days of behind the scenes lobbying of the fifty-seven UN member nations. Each delegate spoke in the debate, sometimes at inordinate length, and observers tallied the likely votes from the indications given in each speech. To pass, the resolution needed a two-thirds majority of the members who voted. As we will see, it got that majority – just – but in a way which was a disgrace to the UN, the new global institution that had been set up to bring peace to the world and prevent conflict.

What happened to destroy the hopes of the Palestinians had been planned for months before the UN vote. A Central Intelligence Agency report on April 1st, 1947, quoted a Jewish Agency representative, Nahum Goldman, saying to the US ambassador in London that "the State Department will be under 'strong pressure' from US Zionists and their friends until the Department takes a line favorable to Zionist aspirations." [147]

The Arab case wasn't helped by the fact that the President of the General Assembly for that session was Oswaldo Aranha, the delegate from Brazil, who was known to have lobbied as fiercely as the Zionists to sway the vote for acceptance of partition. When it seemed likely that that there were not enough votes for partition, Aranha delayed the vote by three days, giving the Zionists extra time to try to make some nations switch their votes, or, as Aranha announced, "in order to make it possible for some measures of conciliation to be taken by interested members."

Here's an example of how the Zionists made use of that time.

Before the delayed vote, the Philippines delegate gave a speech objecting to partition, and explained why:

"My delegation takes part in this final stage in the consideration of the Palestinian problem with profound misgivings. ... We have carefully studied the Report of the Special Committee on Palestine...and pondered the various proposals that have been submitted. As a result of these studies, the Philippines Government has come to the conclusion that it cannot give its support to any proposal for the political disunion and the territorial dismemberment of Palestine ... We hold that the issue is primarily moral. The issue is whether the United Nations should accept responsibility for the enforcement of a policy which, not being mandatory under any specific provision of the Charter, nor in accordance with its fundamental principles, is clearly repugnant to the valid nationalist aspirations of the people of Palestine. The Philippines Government believes that the United Nations ought not to accept any such responsibility." [148]

Any supporters of Palestine hearing that speech would have been pleased to add 'Philippines' to the list of votes against partition. But what happened next dashed their hopes.

Two US Supreme Court justices, friends of the Zionists, Frank Murphy and Felix Frankfurter, contacted the Philippine ambassador in Washington and sent telegrams to Philippine president Manuel Roxas warning that a negative vote would alienate millions of Americans. Ten senators also cabled Roxas. While the Philippine delegate was on his way home on the *Queen Elizabeth,* the Philippine ambassador to the US was on the phone to President Roxas of the Philippines.

"While the Ambassador believed that partition was not wise, he felt that it would be foolish to vote against a policy so ardently desired by the U.S. Administration at a time when seven bills important to the Islands, were pending in the U.S. Congress. The Ambassador and President Roxas agreed that support could be gained easily by voting properly on Palestine." [149]

'Properly' of course, meant doing a 180-degree turn and voting the way the Zionists and the US President wanted.

Another nation strongly against partition was Liberia. We have an account of how their vote was subverted, in a secret Department of State memo, noting a conversation in which the Liberian delegate strongly protested at the pressure that had been imposed to get him to change his vote, after he made an impassioned speech against partition.

"Participant: Gabriel Dennis, Secretary of State of Liberia and delegate to the United Nations General Assembly. State Department, Mr. De La Rue AF

Mr. Dennis said, in fact, that he and the other Liberian delegates, together with a number of delegates from other small countries – he mentioned Haiti specifically – had felt that the plan to partition Palestine, without regard to the wishes of a majority of Palestinian citizens, established a dangerous principle. ... [I]t represented an attempt to avoid the principle of self determination by giving to a minority group a piece of the country, divided on political lines, rather than according to any economic or ethnic basis, and without the consent of a majority of the Palestinian citizens. He said he had opposed this scheme, since he does not believe national entities should be carved up against the wishes of the majority of the people, and he particularly objected to it on the basis that the United Nations, in his opinion, had been created to preserve and defend national integrity and not to act against the wishes of a majority of the people in any country or territory.

He was particularly critical of the action of the members of the United States delegation. He said these had carried on a high-pressure electioneering job, in which they were assisted by the Jewish Agencies and organizations, which had not hesitated to bring pressure on member countries through members of Congress of the United States. He said that in this way, the Liberian minister at Washington [Mr.King] had received a warning that unless Liberia voted with the American delegation in favor of partition, the minister should expect no further favors for his country from Congress. He said, Mr. King, accordingly, had telegraphed the president of Liberia explaining the situation and urging that the President order his delegation at the United Nations to vote for partition. ... The President had wired Mr. Dennis, instructing the delegation to vote with the United States on the subject of partition. Mr. Dennis said they had been most reluctant to do for the reasons first above given, but he had decided they had no choice but to respect the President's orders.

Mr. Dennis also told me that the Haitian delegates had informed him that similar pressures have been used on them, and that the president of Haiti had been advised that if his country needed help from the United States, its vote on this subject would be a material factor in whether or not they got it."[150]

Peter Grose in his book about Israel and America, describes the frenzied activities of the Zionists and their American supporters during the three days of the UN debate:

"To whom would the Liberian delegates really listen? Could anyone reach the Philippines delegation via friends in Manila? How was Haiti leaning on Tuesday? Accosting delegates at every turn, in the lounges at Lake Success, in the diplomatic dining rooms of Manhattan, the Jewish Agency teams deployed all the techniques of persuasion that Weizmann himself had perfected in Balfour's London a generation before. Their arguments were tailored to the interests and emotions of each particular interlocutor. To the diplomats from the Netherlands, the representatives from Jewish Palestine stressed economic development, and praised Dutch efforts at reclamation at home. 'We propose to conquer the wilderness in the same way you conquered the ocean,' argued [David] Horowitz. To the Ethiopians, by contrast, the Zionist team stressed ancient history, the Queen of Sheba, the ties of Ethiopia with the land of Israel in biblical days."[151]

An American journalist, Drew Pearson, explained with pride (he was a Zionist) how the vote had been achieved:

"A lot of people used their influence to whip voters into line. Harvey Firestone, who owns rubber plantations in Liberia, got busy with the Liberian Government. Adolphe Berle, adviser to the President of Haiti, swung that vote... China's Ambassador Wellington Koo warned his government. French Ambassador pleaded with his crisis-laden Government for partition. Few knew it, but President Truman cracked down harder on his State Department than ever before to swing the United Nations vote for the partition of Palestine. Truman called Acting Secretary, Lovett, over to the White House on Wednesday and again on Friday, warning him he would demand a full explanation if nations which usually line up with the United States failed to do so on Palestine. Truman had in mind such countries as Liberia, wholly dependent on the United States; Greece, which would fall overnight without American aid; Haiti, which always follows Washington's lead; and Ethiopia, also indebted to the United States, were stepping out of line on Palestine." [152]

The best and most evocative account I have read of the events surrounding the UN debate itself is a secret report written by a U.K. diplomat, Harold Beeley, a foreign policy adviser to the British Foreign Secretary, Ernest Bevin. Here are some edited extracts from this report:

"It may be that the United Nations will never again be faced with an issue which arouses so intense and local an interest among the population of New York. Throughout the session the delegates, following the Palestine debate in their daily newspapers, had been subjected to the influence of writers who were at once ignorant, prejudiced and unanimous. The cumulative effect of their articles on many Delegates must have been to convey the impression that an opponent of partition was an enemy of the American people. When the final meetings took place in the Assembly hall, the galleries were packed with an almost exclusively Zionist audience. They applauded declarations of support for Zionism. They hissed Arab speakers. They created the atmosphere of a football match, with the Arabs as the away team.

During the closing stages, they came to the conclusion that the partition proposal would still be short of the necessary two-thirds majority in the Assembly. In these circumstances the United States Government was persuaded to use its influence with Governments which were for one reason or another dependent upon it, and which if left to themselves would either vote against partition or abstain. The first symptom … of the American drive for a two-thirds majority was the remark in Mr. Johnson's speech of the 22nd November, that the United States Delegation 'would not understand' abstentions on this important issue'. There then began a movement of small-power Delegations into the partitionist camp. The embarrassment of these repentant sinners was increased by the rapturous welcome each of them received from the New York press, where, however, praise of the United States Government for its efforts still alternated with complaints that it was not being sufficiently energetic. Particularly ludicrous was the position of the Philippine and Haitian Delegates, who were obliged to vote in favour of partition three days after they had spoken against it…

 [The Resolution] was put to the vote, and carried by 33 votes to 13, with 10 abstentions.

The Delegates of Saudi Arabia, Iraq, Syria and the Yemen then made statements to the effect that their Governments did not recognise the validity of the Assembly's decision and reserved their full freedom of action, after which the Arabs walked out of the Assembly."[153]

The whole UN debacle was a classic example of a kangaroo court, defined as "a mock court in which the principles of law and justice are disregarded or perverted". If, in a court of law, a panel of jurors had been treated in the way the Americans treated countries which needed their support, their verdict would have been thrown out. And what is, perhaps, most surprising is that the final vote, with all the manoeuvring of America and the Zionists, was as narrow as it was. If the countries that had changed their votes under pressure had not done so, the resolution would not have passed.

The vote for partition, and therefore for a Jewish state, has since been presented as if it was the result of a massive outpouring of the world's support for a state for the Jewish survivors of Nazi antisemitism, the will of the international community. The Zionist British official, Richard Meinertzhagen wrote:

"[Israel's] origin was ordained by the community of nations. She possesses an international birth certificate such as no other country possesses."[154]

As we've seen, the truth is far more tawdry, and the Palestinians have suffered ever since.

The Palestinian historian, Walid Khalidi has written:

"[Partition] was the ... ostensibly disinterested verdict of an impartial international body. This endowed the concept with the attributes of objectivity and even-handedness – in short of a compromise solution. But a compromise by definition is an arrangement acceptable, however grudgingly, to the protagonists. The 'partition' of Palestine proposed by UNSCOP ... was Zionist in inspiration, Zionist in principle, Zionist in substance, and Zionist in most details. The very idea of partition was abhorrent to the Arabs of Palestine and it was against it that they had fought their bitter, desperate and costly fight in the years 1937-9. Also, 'compromise' implies mutual concession. What were the Zionists conceding? You can only really concede what you possess. What possessions in Palestine were the Zionists conceding? None at all."[155]

There is a letter which puzzles me in the Zionist archives from Chaim Weizmann to President Truman. It is written from the Plaza, one of New York's most expensive hotels, and in it, perhaps evincing his inner Captain Renault*, Weizmann says

> "I am disturbed to hear from unimpeachable sources that two unwarranted rumours are afloat which do us injustice and possible damage. It is freely rumoured in Washington that our people have exerted undue and excessive pressure on certain delegations and have thus "overplayed" their hand. I cannot speak for unauthorised persons, but I am in a position to assure you, my dear Mr. President, that there is no substance in this charge as far as our representatives are concerned. They have had a very limited number of contacts with all delegations and have endeavoured to lay the situation squarely before them. At no time have they gone beyond the limits of legitimate and moderate persuasion. With some delegations such as those of Greece and Liberia, we had had no more than one conversation throughout the present Assembly."[156]

I can only assume that Weizmann is taking refuge in literalism and hopes that, if challenged on his use of the phrase 'our people' he would have pleaded that he meant something like 'salaried members of the Zionist Organisation' rather than Zionists in general. Certainly, if Weizmann's letter is correct, the accounts of the events by Harold Beeley and Drew Pearson are fabrications.

But what I find puzzling is not the denials but why Weizmann needs to tell Truman something they both know to be untrue. Truman in his memoirs reveals this:

> "The facts were that not only were there pressure movements around the United Nations unlike anything that had been seen there before, but that the White House, too, was subjected to a constant barrage. I do not think I ever had as much pressure and propaganda aimed at the White House as I had in this instance. The persistence of a few of the extreme Zionist leaders—actuated by political motives and engaging in political threats—disturbed and annoyed me."[157]

---

* "I'm shocked! shocked! to be accused of pressuring the UN delegates."

Perhaps Weizmann's letter was the sort of thing people write to cover their backs, although far too many people knew and wrote about the truth for it to be much use for that purpose. Gideon Rafael, a Jewish Agency member, recalled:

"It was a very exciting period. We were on the go day and night. We didn't just report at these meetings. There was also an operational division of assignments: 'You work on these delegations,' 'You on those.' We discussed the weak points and where we had to mobilize influence in various capitals."[158]

While the Zionist pressure was all to achieve partition, this was a policy decision taken with an ulterior motive. Ever since Ben-Gurion – as he claimed – suggested the idea to the Peel Commission, it was not because the Zionists had had a rush to the head of reasonableness, or a belief that they really should share the land with the Palestinian Arabs. As Ben-Gurion explained in an internal discussion as far back as 1938, "after we become a strong force, as a result of the creation of a state, we shall abolish partition and expand into the whole of Palestine."[159]

Chaim Weizmann echoed this when he said:

"It is our destiny to get Palestine and this destiny will be fulfilled someday somehow. Our present task is to get a fulcrum on which to place a lever, and if we are capable, within the area allotted to us, of bringing in 50,000 or 60,000 Jews a year for the next 20 years or so, then our job is to make the best of such an opportunity in our own house, with our own forces, as a small sovereign State, leaving the problems of expansion and extension to future generations. There is no absolute in this world; everything is a flux."[160]

The world has had many opportunities over the last 75 years to see exactly how the Zionist successors of Ben-Gurion and Weizmann handled 'problems of expansion and extension' at the expense of the Palestinian people.

Chapter 9: Mayhem

The UN vote for partition was held on November 29th, 1947. Between that date and May 14th, 1948, when the British withdrew from Palestine, the Palestinian Arabs saw the nature of the people who claimed publicly to want to live side with them in peace and cooperation. There had been ongoing attacks on the British in the 1940s in Palestine by Jewish terrorist organisations, supported covertly by politicians and the 'official' Jewish army, Haganah, but now, increasingly, it was Arabs who were the focus of Jewish terror.

It seemed that Ben-Gurion's plan to "abolish partition and expand into the whole of Palestine" was being put in action before even partition had occurred. In fact, Ben-Gurion had overseen the drawing up of a plan, Plan D or 'Dalet' in Hebrew, in 1946, and its final details were ready to be put into operation later in 1947. In the words of the Israeli historian, Ilan Pappé, "Plan Dalet called for the systematic and total expulsion [of Palestinians] from their homeland."[a]

Walid Khalidi describes in more detail how it would work:

"Plan Dalet's … overriding objective was the seizure and retention of territory. The minimum area to be seized was, of course, that assigned to the Jewish State. But certain Jewish settlements … lay outside the area of the Jewish state and these had to be 'defended'. The Jewish sector of Jerusalem lay in the middle of the proposed Arab state and this was 'undesirable'. Jewish settlements in the plains were 'dominated' by Arab villages on higher ground, and these villages, although in the proposed Arab state, presented a 'security threat' to the Jewish settlements. The area of the Jewish state proposed by the UN partition plan had already been described by Zionist leaders as the 'irreducible minimum'. There was no telling what Plan Dalet would yield in terms of territory, since the Arabs were resisting partition and by so doing inviting 'retaliation'. But there was one constraint - the time factor. Plan Dalet should achieve its principal objectives before or by 15 May 1948. On that day … the British Mandate would end and a juridical vacuum would be created in Palestine unless it was filled by the military fait accompli of the rise of Israel." [162]

It's worth taking in precisely what Plan Dalet was proposing and how outrageous it was.

At the time of the UN vote, the country had a 'mixed' population of Palestinians and Jews, although in terms of land possession the word 'mixed' is misleading since the Jews owned only 6% or 7% of land in 1947. Although the Jewish Agency had tried to persuade immigrant Jews to settle in the countryside, most were unwilling to do so and preferred to settle in towns and cities. Those who did settle in the country set up isolated colonies which were effectively islands in the Palestinian Arab countryside.

Plan Dalet's aim of 'defending' Jewish colonies in the area allocated to Palestinians Arabs, long before the British left Palestine, was effectively a licence to attack surrounding villages and communities which 'might be' a threat. You might call it 'pre-retaliation', a technique which Israel has used ever since to justify attacks on Palestinians in Gaza and the West Bank.

Throughout 1947, Palestinian Arabs suffered the effect of a series of unprovoked attacks in what was effectively a war by the Zionists against Palestinian Arabs.

I say 'unprovoked' because there was nothing the Palestinians did to cause the grievance that led to the Zionists' attacking them. Whoever's fault it was that there were hundreds of thousands of Palestinians living in places the Jews wanted for their state, outside the Jewish area in the partition plan, it wasn't the Palestinians'. Nevertheless, as Plan Dalet swung into action, it was they who suffered.

So far in this book I have tried to show how the Palestinians were subjected to *political* violence, as I would call it, for twenty years.

The Balfour Declaration was imposed upon them, followed by Jewish immigration without their consent, the denial of the self-determination they had been entitled to expect, the misuse of the Holocaust survivors to gather world support for Zionism, and the gift of more than half their land by a world that didn't own it to a people who had no right to it.

110

Now, in 1947, under Plan Dalet, they were to be subject to a campaign of *physical* violence against men, women and children which left them in no doubt that their entire existence – wherever they lived in Palestine – was under threat from Zionism,

A bare catalogue of some of the violence perpetrated against Palestinians in the months leading up to the day the British abandoned Palestine makes for chilling reading.

In August 1947, Haganah, the 'official' Jewish militia, blew up a house near Jaffa, killing 11 Arabs including 4 children. The following day, Haganah attacked the Arab village of Qazaza, near the Jewish town of Rehoboth, for three hours. The house of the village mukhtar (headman) was dynamited 'with the people inside' according to a Haganah spokesman. The Jewish Agency issued a statement commending the Haganah raids, describing the killing of the five small children as 'very unfortunate'.

On the 29th September, the Irgun used a barrel bomb to kill 12 people, including six Palestinians, and injure 54. Thomas Suarez in his book, *State of Terror*, says of this event:

"'The general reaction' of the Jewish settlements to the massacre, according to a military report, 'was one of admiration for the way the outrage was implemented and very little sympathy was reserved for the dead and wounded'."[163]

Suarez described other atrocities:

"At about 10:15 on the night of 6 October, between fifteen and twenty militants approached two Palestinian tents, and indiscriminately opened fire into the tents with 160 rounds…. Neighbouring Palestinians fled for safety, but the attackers killed two more in their escape."[164]

Of course, once it was clear what danger every Palestinian was in, there were attempts by individual Palestinians to defend themselves, with far less access to guns and bombs than the Zionists with their huge armories of smuggled weapons. But Arab violence was minimal compared with the onslaughts of Irgun and Haganah. This didn't suit the Zionist plan at all, as Suarez observes:

"Disappointment among Zionist leaders, whose plans to conquer Palestine in the name of self-defence required an 'Arab threat', was sufficiently visible that it was noted in a British military report for the fortnight ending 10 October:

'The Jews continue to exhibit signs of anxiety because the lack of [Palestinian] disturbances shows unexpected control by the Arab leaders over the masses.'

Whether or not 'the Jews' were correct in attributing 'the lack of disturbances' to 'Arab leaders', the Palestinians were not responding to the violence."[165]

On the 18th December, Haganah, the 'official' Jewish militia, staged a raid on the Arab village of Khisas in retaliation for the killing of two Jewish policemen on the road within five miles of the village. The attack started at 9 p.m. with two carloads of men driving through the village, firing rifles and machine-guns, and throwing grenades as they went. Two houses were demolished by explosives. In the wreckage, the police next day found five dead Arab children. Total Arab casualties were ten dead and five injured. None of them had been involved in the killing of the Jewish police.

On New Year's day, 1948, Jews raided two Arab villages, killed ten Arabs in a Jaffa café, and blew up the Jaffa-Tel Aviv railroad. Two days later, the Arab Higher Committee's Jaffa office was destroyed by the Stern Gang, dressed as Arabs, by detonating high explosives in a parked truck, an explosion which killed 14 Arabs and wounded 98. In the Katamon quarter of Jerusalem, Haganah members blew up the Arab-owned Semiramis Hotel, alleged by them to be the Arab military headquarters, killing 20 Arabs and the Spanish Acting-Consul, and wounding 12 others.

On the 18th January, 1948, Jewish terrorists demolished twelve buildings in Jaffa with high explosives and attacked three Arab villages in Hebron; and on 19th January, in their first 'air-raid', three Jewish planes attacked Gaza railway station, dropping bombs which killed nine members of the railway staff, including the station-master. These later attacks couldn't even use the excuse of reprisals but were designed to warn and intimidate.

Also in January, Haifa was almost completely paralysed in 'a day of terror and near anarchy' as all transport ceased after nineteen Arab buses had been destroyed by Zionists, and both Jews and Arabs took to sniping along the streets. "Jewish sources in Haifa accused the British troops and police of standing by and that the army convoyed workers home and aided the wounded," the *New York Times* correspondent reported, "The overall picture, however, is one of Jewish rather than Arab attack" and the day after this dispatch the Jews exploded land-mines in the Arab district of Haifa, and claimed 82 Arabs killed in 24 hours. (In one house, eight children were killed and four wounded.)[166]

Walid Khalidi comments:

"Zero-hour for Plan Dalet was 1 April 1948. Thirteen operations were carried out within this plan's framework. There were only six weeks to go. Hence the merciless fury of the assaults. The greatest Arab asset was that they were there, on site, in their towns and villages. But this was the historic opportunity to de-Arabize the land of Israel, to negate Arab presence by simply removing it, to solve with a few crushing blows all the problems presented by the fact that, in the UN proposed Jewish state, the Arabs were equal in number to the Jews and owned the bulk of the land. Plan Dalet was conducted on two levels, the military and psychological."[167]

Remember, these atrocities were taking place while the Palestine was still under the Administration that had ruled the country for the last thirty years. Britain was still nominally in charge of the whole of Palestine. War had not yet broken out in any formal sense and Arabs throughout Palestine were entitled to the protection of the Administration. But the Jewish militias and terrorists gangs knew that they could act with impunity against the Palestinians – the heart had gone out of any British response – and Walid Khalidi describes the result:

> "The Palestinian Arabs broke under the full impact of Plan Dalet. The combination of military and psychological techniques produced a panic of mass proportions. The inhabitants of the coastal towns, Jaffa, Haifa and Acre, cut off from their hinterlands, were literally thrown into the sea. Hundreds of men, women and children were drowned in the scramble under fire for any vessel or fishing craft to take them to safety. A vast exodus of hundreds of thousands of refugees was driven before the victorious Jewish brigades across the borders. Plan Dalet was supremely successful and the road was open for the restoration of the historical frontiers of Israel in the whole country. Already by 23 April, and with the fall of Haifa, it was clear that Plan Dalet had achieved its purpose."[168]

During April 1948, eight out of thirteen major Zionist attacks on Arabs occurred in the territory granted to the Arab state. They included a huge attack on the Arab city of Jaffa, two weeks before the Mandate ended, starting with a three-day mortar bombardment and then an invasion by 600 members of Irgun. The citizens of Jaffa did their best to defend themselves but the imbalance of weaponry made it impossible, and many Palestinians lost everything. In the words of the Anglo-Jewish journalist Jon Kimche, "Everything that was moveable was carried off from Jaffa – furniture, carpets, pictures, crockery and pottery, jewelry and cutlery. The occupied part of Jaffa was stripped ... what could not be taken away was smashed. Windows, pianos, fittings and lamps went in an orgy of destruction."[169]

Zionists are fond of saying that in 1948, the Arabs wanted to push the Jews into the sea. Like so much in this story, the truth is the reverse. In Jaffa, surrounded by Jewish forces, the only way to avoid being killed for many Palestinians was to head for the sea, where many of them drowned

The war between the Arabs and the Jews did not begin on the day the state of Israel was declared – it raged, very one-sidedly, for the last six months of British 'control' of Palestine.

And sitting on the sidelines were the surrounding Arab states, observing that what they had feared for their Palestinian brethren was happening, and they could do nothing about it. For the British, of course, were nominally in charge, and along with the US they pressured the leaders of the Arab countries not to invade Palestine.

On May 2nd, less than two weeks before the British withdrawal, the UK Colonial Secretary, Arthur Creech-Jones, wrote to the US Secretary of State:

"I appreciate the continued pressure which you have been bringing to bear on the Arab States in order to prevent precipitate action by them before 15th May *and understand how provocative to the Arabs Jewish operations in Palestine have been* [my italics]. I can only stress again that it is important, from the point of view of our international obligations as seen at Lake Success that we continue to exercise our influence on the Arabs that they show all possible restraint. Speculation here is particularly rife as regards our policy towards Transjordan and the Arab Legion. Any move by Abdullah before 15th May would react seriously to our prejudice and, even after 15th May, intervention by Transjordan is likely to create a most embarrassing situation for His Majesty's Government."[170]

Provocative, indeed. Before May 15th, 1948, the Jews had occupied most of the Arab cities in Palestine. Tiberias was occupied on April 19, Haifa on April 22, Jaffa on April 28, the Arab quarters in the New City of Jerusalem on April 30, Beisan on May 8, Safad on May 10 and Acre on May 14, 1948. In contrast, the Palestine Arabs did not seize any of the territories reserved for the Jewish state under the partition resolution.[171]

And yet, the Arab armies, provoked both by the Jewish onslaughts on Palestinians and by the swelling numbers of Palestinians fleeing to their countries, were able to do nothing for the Palestinian Arabs while the British still occupied Palestine. A series of confidential CIA reports describe the cautious deliberations among the other Arab states:

April 22nd: Increasing Arab pressure for intervention – US Chargé Memminger in Damascus reports that pressure from the

Arab press and public for the active intervention of the Arab state armies in Palestine is growing stronger daily.

27 April 1948: Arab plans for intervention developing slowly – Reports from US and UK diplomatic representatives in Arab capitals indicate that despite tremendous public pressure for intervention, responsible Arab leaders are apprehensive of committing their regular armies in Palestine. The King of Transjordan and the Regent of Iraq are said to have insisted that before they move their troops assurances must be given by all Arab states of full support with men, money, and materials. The Egyptian Government is reluctant to participate in such a campaign because of probable international repercussions and the need of retaining all its forces in Egypt for reasons of internal security.

April 30, 1948: Developments in Palestine situation – US Ambassador Douglas in London ... says that the replies of the Arab governments indicate that if the Jewish forces desist from provocative attacks and aggressive action against Arab areas in Palestine, the Arab states will not engage in offensive military operations. Several of the governments point out, however, that because the Jews are on the offensive everywhere, it will be difficult for the Arab forces to refrain from engaging in "retaliatory action."

May 3, 1948: Arab invasion of Palestine unlikely before 15 May – US Ambassador Wadsworth in Baghdad has been informed by the Transjordan Minister to Iraq that at the recent conference at Amman, 5 May was not set as D-day for the Arab invasion of Palestine. According to the Transjordan Minister, it was agreed at Amman that: (a) the Transjordan Arab Legion would not invade Palestine "in force" until after 15 May; and (b) other Arab states would maintain contingents along the frontiers but would not invade Palestine unless the Arab Legion failed or unless "there should be intervention by a foreign power."

May 5, 1948: McMillan considers it "not unlikely" that Transjordan troops will move into the Arab areas of Palestine after the mandate ends but believes that King Abdullah will avoid risking his army in battle with the Jews.

May 10, 1948: The US Military Attaché in Damascus transmits the opinion ... that the general impression of informed observers is that Abdullah will in effect implement partition by occupying only the Arab sections of Palestine and restoring order.

May 11, 1948: [Ernest] Bevin adds his belief that although King Abdullah's exact intentions are not known, if the Transjordan Legion should move into Palestine at all, it would only occupy legitimate and clearly recognized Arab positions.   Bevin expresses the hope that both Arabs and Jews will keep out of each other's areas and thereby prepare for a natural "sorting out of Palestine" and an effective truce, under which the Arabs and Jews might provide separate militias for the maintenance of order and administration.[172]

It's time to take a breather, because we have reached a crucial stage in this sad story. I started this book by analysing the canard that 'Arab armies invaded Israel' on May 15th 1948. In the next chapter I will describe what actually happened on that day, but there is a clue in those few CIA messages, secret at the time and so hardly to be treated as someone's propaganda.   No one is talking about the Arab armies invading the *Jewish state*. The only invasion that is discussed is an invasion of *Palestine,* and some messages make clear that that refers to the Arab areas only.

Some Palestinians whose lives were to be changed irrevocably by the "Jewish National Home"

117

"The predominant single image of the war in the Western mind is that of a tiny, poorly armed and pacific Israel attacked in its cradle and without provocation by the overwhelming force of the regular armies of the neighboring Arab states."[173]

I started this book with the false quotes about the actions of the Arab armies on May 15th. I have tried to show the accumulation of causes of anger and fear among Palestinians over the twenty years from the time they were told by the British government that their land would be turned into a Jewish state. Whoever they spoke to in power and whatever they said, it became clear that the British listened to only one voice – Dr Weizmann and his friends. Remember Churchill – "You are our master"?

The rising anger in Palestine and among its Arab allies, countries which, unlike Palestine, had been granted their well-deserved independence, could well have turned into a determination to attack the Jewish state when it was formed and – as is often claimed was their intention – to 'push the Jews into the sea'. Whether or not they had the soldiers and weapons to do so – in fact the Jews had superiority in both – that might not have stopped them. The Arabs have often shown the triumph of heart over head in the decisions they have made. But for whatever reason, and in spite of what Israel wants people to believe, they did not invade Israel. They no more invaded Israel than Britain and the Americans invaded Germany on D-Day. The Allies invaded France, and the Arab armies entered – not invaded – Palestine, as they were entitled to do after the end of the British Mandate.

The Israeli historian Avi Shlaim writes:

"The conventional Zionist version portrays the 1948 war as a simple, bipolar no-holds-barred struggle between a monolithic Arab adversary and a tiny Israel. According to this version, seven Arab armies invaded Palestine upon expiration of the British mandate with a single aim in mind: to strangle the Jewish state as soon as it came into the world. The subsequent struggle was an unequal one between a Jewish David and an Arab Goliath. The infant Jewish state fought a desperate, heroic, and ultimately successful battle for survival against overwhelming odds. During the war hundreds of thousands of Palestinians fled to the neighbouring Arab states, mainly in response to orders from their leaders and in the expectation of a triumphal return. After the war, the story continues, Israel's leaders sought peace with all their heart and all their might, but there was no one to talk with on the other side. Arab intransigence was alone responsible for the political deadlock that persisted for three decades after the guns fell silent. This popular-heroic-moralistic version of the 1948 war has been used extensively in Israeli propaganda and is still taught in Israeli schools. It is a prime example of the use of a nationalist version of history in the process of nation building. In a very real sense history is the propaganda of the victors, and the history of the 1948 war is no exception." [174]

The Arab armies were no threat. At all times during the fighting, the IDF significantly outnumbered all the Arab forces arrayed against it, and by the final stage of the war its superiority ratio was nearly two to one. The Palestinians themselves entered the fighting "with a deeply divided leadership, exceedingly limited finances, no centrally organized military forces or centralized administrative organs, and no reliable allies. They faced a Jewish society in Palestine which, although small relative to theirs, was politically unified, had centralized para-state institutions, and was exceedingly well led and extremely highly motivated." [175]

The Zionists had a further advantage. While the Arab countries were prevented from acquiring weapons by an arms embargo operated by UN member countries, the Soviet bloc did not observe this. The Jews received a massive supply of heavy arms, tanks, and planes through Czechoslovakia, after the Communist takeover in March 1948.

On May 12th, two days before the British left, the US Ambassador to the UK sent a cable to the US Secretary of State:

"Following is attempt synthesise current thinking re Palestine of foreign office officials with whom Embassy officer has talked

119

during past few days. The consensus of their views seems to be that (A) [King] Abdullah [of Jordan] is only positive factor Arab side. Arab Higher Committee, Mufti, and Arab governments for various reasons do not show signs of assuming significant roles next few weeks, although Iraq and Egypt might arrange to fire a few token shots just to be able to say they have done so. (B) Abdullah will stop without attacking at any point which would involve fighting with Jews i.e. substantially at frontier of Jewish states."[176]

John Glubb, the British officer who led the Jordanian Arab Legion.

Abdullah's army, the Arab Legion, commanded by a British officer, John Glubb, was the most significant Arab force in the fighting. But there was one factor in the Jordanian strategy which didn't come to light until much later.

"The Jordanian Arab Legion and the Iraqi army, which was under Jordanian command, never crossed the partition lines because of strict British orders to that effect, and a prior understanding with the Jewish Agency that Amir Abdullah negotiated with Moshe Shertok (later Sharrett) and Golda Meir." [177]

That needs to be read carefully to understand its significance. *Jewish representatives had met Abdullah in secret as part of a plan to allow Abdullah to acquire for Jordan the territory allocated to the Palestinian Arabs.* Israeli sources have denied that there was any formal agreement between Abdullah and the Jews, but a secret report by a Jewish official at the meeting shows that the Jews were happy to go along with what Abdullah proposed – the acquisition of the Arab part of Palestine for his own state, in return for confining his activities to the rest of Palestine rather than attacking the new Jewish state:

> "At this point [Abdullah] went on to ask what our attitude would be to an attempt by him to seize the Arab part of the country? We replied that we would look favourably on it, especially if it did not obstruct us in the establishment of our state, did not lead to a confrontation between us and his forces, and, particularly if this action were accompanied by a declaration that the seizure was solely aimed at ensuring order and keeping the peace until the United Nations could establish a government in that part [of Palestine]"[178]

Another report said that the Jews were:

> "...prepared to acquiesce in his capture of these areas – but only as a temporary law-enforcement measure to prevent bloodshed and facilitate the establishment of a legitimate Palestinian government in accordance with the UN Partition Resolution."[179]

A large pinch of salt needs to be taken with that last assertion. As we have seen, nothing was further from the Zionists' thought than 'the establishment of a legitimate Palestinian government.'

Once again we are confronted with a piece of research that gives the lie to the 'David and Goliath' myth of Israel and the Arabs. Six months before Arab armies (didn't) invade Israel, senior figures in the future Jewish government knew that the Jordanian army, the force that would have posed the biggest threat, had its own reasons for not crossing the border of what was to become Israel. Knowing that would have given the Jews *carte blanche* for their attacks on the Palestinian Arabs who, if they had known of Abdullah's intentions, might well have objected to becoming Jordanians rather than Palestinians.

The 'five Arab armies' myth implies some kind of coordinated Arab military response in May 1948. While efforts were made to synchronise the activities of the various armies, in fact, as often happened before and after 1948, the Arab states were at loggerheads with each other, and in this case, since Abdullah's aims might clash with the others', the Israelis knew more about his plans than Syria, Egypt, Iraq and Lebanon.

A 'most secret' report by Brigadier-General Sir Iltyd Clayton, British Public Liaison Officer to the British Ambassador in Cairo, reported on a conversation with the prime minister of Jordan in December, 1947, five months before the non-invasion of Israel:

> "The Transjordan Government will announce the advance of the Arab Legion into Palestine under the pretext to save it from the Zionists … This action should not raise the suspicions of the Arab States. … As a town or area is occupied, this will be attached to the territory of Transjordan, it being understood that only the area allotted to the Arab State under the partition plan will be so attached. The Prime Minister assured me that the Arab Legion will not attack any Jewish settlement except that 'make believe' attacks will be made in order to remove any suspicions. As soon as the territory reserved for the Arab State has been occupied, the Trans-Jordan Government will contact the Jewish leaders requesting guarantees that they will at no time attempt to expand the boundaries of their state or invade the Arab villages on the borders." [180]

Whether or not the Jews actually made a binding agreement with Abdullah – the subject of academic controversy because no such written agreement exists – there were Jewish officials at the time who accepted that they had to agree a *quid pro quo* for Abdullah's agreement not to attack Israel. Yaacov Shimoni, in the Political Department of the Jewish Agency, wrote:

> "We would agree to the conquest of the Arab part of Palestine by 'Abdullah. We would not stand in his way. We would not help him, would not seize it and hand it over to him. He would have to take it by his own means and stratagems but we would not disturb him. He, for his part, would not prevent us from

establishing the state of Israel, from dividing the country, taking our share and establishing a state in it."[181]

While the facts about Jordan's future restraint were known to the Zionists, this didn't stop them using scare tactics in the United Nations. On April 22nd 1948, Abba Silver addressed delegates in the UN General Assembly:

"Seated around this table are representatives of Arab States whose governments pledged themselves to observe the letter and the spirit of the Charter and who have, by their own admissions, called for violent resistance to the decision of the United Nations, armed and equipped bands of their nationals who proceeded to cross the frontiers into Palestine to carry death and destruction to the inhabitants of that country. They are at this very moment preparing for even larger military action upon the termination of the mandate, if not sooner. This clearly is not merely non-acceptance of a General Assembly recommendation. This is brazen and contemptuous violation of the United Nations Charter, which calls upon its member states to refrain from the threat or use of force in international relations. The representatives of these states, who have flaunted [sic] the United Nations, are here today counseling this international organization, whose authority and prestige they have trampled underfoot, to sanction their aggression and to reward their violence by repudiating a decision which had been overwhelmingly adopted and to substitute for it a solution which would be entirely acceptable to them. This indeed is an incredible spectacle astounding, sinister, ominous."[182]

(If any trampling underfoot of the United Nations is involved it is Israel over the last 75 years which has done the trampling. As mentioned earlier, the UN General Assembly resolutions are not binding on members[183]. What *are* binding are UN Security Council resolutions, and since the Israel joined the UN it has ignored scores of them. The list begins Resolution 242 (196), Resolution 338 (1973), Resolution 446 (1979), Resolution 478 (1980) … and on and on through the following 24 years.)

123

While Jordan's Arab Legion was the most formidable and best trained of the Arab armies, it was no real threat to Israel because of the implicit agreement between the two parties. Conversely, while other Arab armies took part, they varied from the barely effective to the incompetent, hampered by limited supplies of weapons.

The Lebanese units, for most of the war, were happy to remain on their side of the border with Palestine, where they reluctantly tried to defend the adjacent villages. The Iraqi troops numbered a few thousand and had been ordered by their government to accept the Jordanian guideline: that is, not to attack the Jewish state, but just to defend the area King Abdullah wanted, namely the West Bank. They were stationed in the northern part of the West Bank. However, they defied their politicians' orders and tried to play a more effective role. Because of this, fifteen villages in the Palestinian Arab partition area were able to resist Jewish attacks and thus escape expulsion. For three weeks these Arab units – some provoked into action by their politicians' hypocrisy, others deterred by it – succeeded in entering and holding on to the areas the UN Partition Resolution had allocated to the Arab state. In a few places they were able to encircle isolated Jewish settlements located in the Arab areas and occupy them for a while, only to lose them again within a few days.

This account has barely scraped the surface of the complex events in the first half of 1948. But I hope I have shown enough to establish that five Arab armies did not invade Israel, and that May 15th was not the point where the Arab-Israeli war began, but that it had raged for more than six months before that date and consisted of the Jewish forces attacking Arabs by invading territories that were *outside* the area allocated to the Jewish state.

One simple indication of the extent to which it was the Jewish forces which breached the partition borders rather than the Arabs was that 60% of the Jewish soldiers who were killed in action, were killed in attacks in the areas allotted by the UN to the Palestinians.[184]

One final visual confirmation of the points I have been making in this chapter, comes in the endpapers of a book published in 1950, called *New Star in the Near East*, by an American, Kenneth W. Bilby, which praises the heroic efforts of the Jews to establish the state of Israel in the face of overwhelming odds.

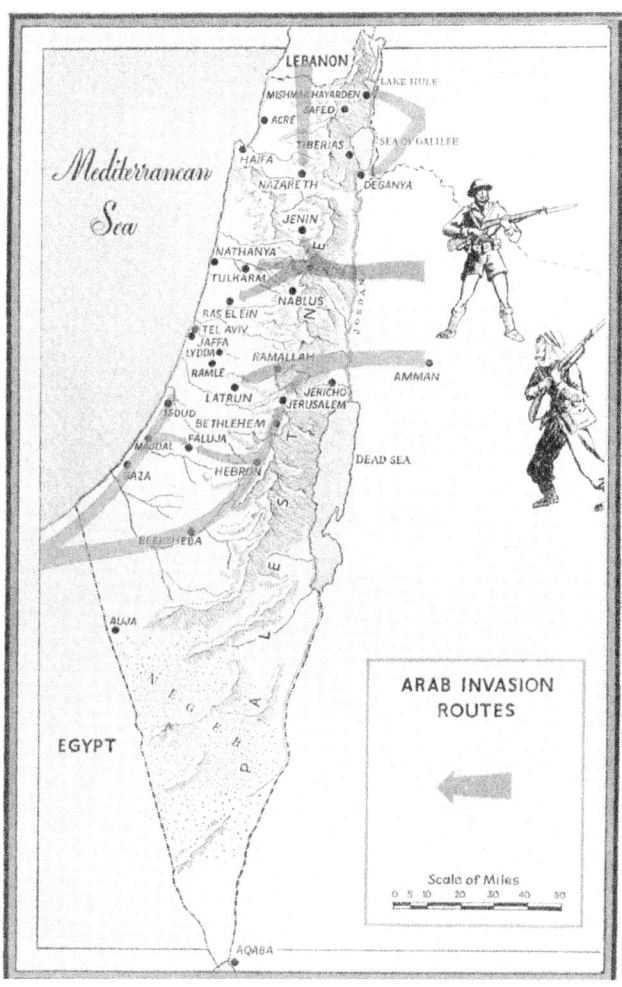

This map encapsulates the entire argument I am trying to make about Israel's biggest lie. To the uninformed reader the map shows the terrifying sight of five Arab armies 'invading Israel'. The thick grey arrows from north, east and south represent the Arab armies. Surely, if this map is accurate, no one can deny the facts of the invasion. However, as we have seen I *do* deny those facts. The map *is* accurate, apart from the fact that the Lebanese army didn't take part, but the armies are not invading Israel. To show why, in the next map I have superimposed the boundaries of the areas allocated to the Jews and the Arabs.

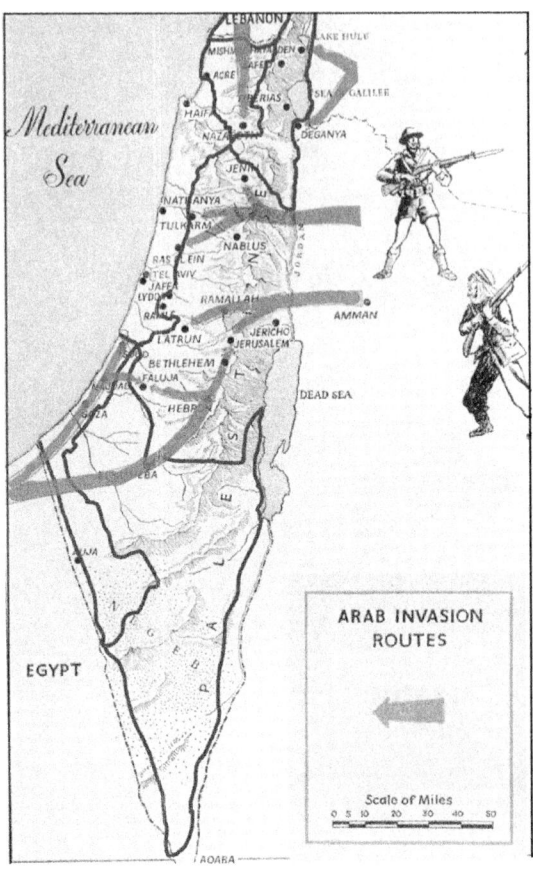

Although I have not labelled the thick black lines, you can tell which is the area allocated to the Jews because, apart from one exception, *there are no arrows* in the area that was about to become Israel. Mr Bilby, of course, does not show the UN partition boundaries because they would entirely destroy the case that "on May 15th, five Arab armies invaded Israel."

The only Arab army that did make some attempt to attack the new state was the Egyptian army. As we've seen, before May 15th Zionist militias had already invaded, ethnically cleansed, and conquered vast swathes of the area allocated to the Arab state, and Egypt retaliated by a short bombing campaign on Tel Aviv, and by crossing the Negev, allocated to the Jews, to reach Beersheba, an Arab town in the Palestinian Arab area. Their ire against the new Jewish state was aggravated by the discovery that a Haganah division had entered Gaza, an Arab area under Egyptian control, and put two cans of typhus and dysentery into the water supply.

Kenneth Bilby himself, in spite of his misleading map, filled in some details:

> "I was in the Jewish section of Jerusalem with a dozen other British and American correspondents when the mandate ended. We were trapped without adequate communications and unable to get through the ring the Legion had forged around the New City. Each night we picked up Arab radio broadcasts, about our only link with the outside world, and those from Cairo were wondrous indeed. The Egyptian Army, according to Cairo radio, had just crossed the Sinai desert and was chalking up an unparalleled string of victories. It had taken Beersheba (but Beersheba was an Arab town, occupied by its Arab inhabitants); the column which moved up the coast had occupied Gaza (another Arab town); had overrun El Majdal and Isdud (two more Arab towns) and was now less than twenty miles from Tel Aviv."[185]

The message of this chapter is not that the Arab states, and the Palestinians, were not hostile to the Jews. Far from it. I have shown earlier how many reasons Palestinians had for mistrusting and then hating the Zionist movement and its attempts to take their land. But the need for Israel and its supporters to demonise, denigrate, and dominate the Palestinians over twenty years, to exaggerate the threat from them in 1948 and invent a fictional invasion by Arab armies when they were no threat at all, suggests a degree of guilt about the whole Zionist enterprise. If the case for a Jewish state in Palestine was a valid one it should stand on its merits. Indeed, instead of enlisting Britain – by lying of course – in the project, why not approach the Palestinians directly, and with a less dogmatic statement of their case, perhaps aiming for a safe haven for those Jews who wanted to go there, not insisting on a state for the entire world's Jews? They might even have approached the task through the Jewish community in Palestine that had already lived peaceably side by side with Arab Palestinians for a century or more. But any agreement that might have emerged from such an approach could have required a degree of compromise from the Zionists which would have clashed with their insistence on a Jewish state 'as Jewish as England is English.'

Chapter 11: Epilogue

Palestinians and their advocates are often criticised for 'dwelling on the past.' But the existence of Israel itself is a prime example of what dwelling on the past can achieve. Four thousand years is a pretty long period to dwell on, and yet the arguments presented for a Jewish claim on Palestine are based on patchy residence by some Jews in Palestine for periods scattered throughout that period and, notably, hardly at all during the recent centuries when the population was almost entirely Arab. And of course, there is the fact that the connection between Jews today and any Jews who lived in Palestine thousands of years ago is more sentimental than biological.

In this last chapter of this book I want to address one specific aspect of 'dwelling on the past' – the issue of whether the way Zionism treated Palestinians between 1917 and 1947 tells us anything about the nature of the state of Israel from 1948 till today. As we've seen, the Zionists of the first half of the twentieth century used racist arguments, lies, threats, bribes, and violence to force their case in front of the world's leaders, most notably in Britain and America, as well as using terrorism on the Palestinians themselves. But having achieved their aim in 1948, from then on a new generation of Jews could have decided to behave differently, to observe the norms of international diplomacy and governance and behave to its non-Jewish citizens and its Arab neighbours with some kind of honesty, justice and benevolence. It was, after all, the Jews who took Arab land, not the other way round. And since five Arab armies did *not* invade Israel, there isn't even the excuse of unprovoked aggression to justify continuing hostility to Palestinians by Israel.

I'm going to take just one of the inexcusable elements of Zionist policy used against Palestinians during the time of the Mandate – unjustifiable violence – and suggest that there has been no change from the policy adapted by the Zionist political movement to acquire a Jewish state, and the continued stance of the government of that state after its independence was achieved.

I should say that I have tried in this book to distinguish between Zionist Jews and others. There have always been Jews who do not agree with the aims and behaviour of Zionists. At the time of the Balfour Declaration, there was a significant body of English Jews who objected to the activities of Weizmann and Balfour. In the 1930s, leading Jews in Palestine like Judah Magnes tried to put an argument for the Jews sharing Palestine with its indigenous inhabitants. Even in the Displaced Persons camps, there was a significant proportion of Jews who disagreed with the 'Jewish state' idea, members of a political grouping called the Bund. And I know today there are Israeli Jews who hate what is done in their name, and do their best to draw attention to Israel's inhuman treatment of Palestinians. Some of them are quoted in this book.

What puzzles me most about Israel's attitude to the Palestinians is not the country's continual use of lying as a political tool – many governments massage the truth in public –, or its racism – again, prejudice is endemic in a number of so called civilised countries, but its addiction to violence, the tool which more than any other caused the British to abandon the Mandate, and the Palestinians to flee their own land.

There are two types of Jewish violence which occurred in 1940s Palestine. One could be seen – charitably – as an instrument of war. All countries in wartime reserve the right to attack people they see as their opponents, and long before 1948, the Palestinians were seen as opponents of the Jews. Sometimes they actually were, attacking Jewish positions because of threats of Jewish violence, or retaliating for some action which might itself be claimed by the Jews as a retaliation for Arab actions. The claim that Jewish aggression before 1948 was in any sense legitimate warfare is a shaky one but nevertheless, encounters took place that had the appearance of warfare.

The second type of violence was terrorism – the attacking, killing, maiming and destruction inflicted by Jews on

Palestinians whose only offense was that they wished to live where their families had lived for generations rather than hand over land, homes and possession to Jews.

There is one classic example which for years after 1948 was labelled as Arab propaganda until the evidence was too voluminous to deny. It was the destruction of the inhabitants of a village called Deir Yassin, in the outskirts of Jerusalem, by a Jewish terrorist group called the Irgun. There are many detailed accounts of this event but I will summarise the consequences. There were a minimum of 107 people killed, including many women and children. These were not just 'clean' deaths, by shooting for example, but included vicious and sadistic torture.

A British CID inspector wrote:

"There is … no doubt that many sexual atrocities were committed by the attacking [Zionists]. Many young school-girls were raped and later slaughtered. Old women were also molested. One story is current concerning a case in which a young girl was literally torn into two. Many infants were also butchered and killed."[186]

A Mossad intelligence officer reported:

"We witnessed a most horrible and dreadful scene…. [Irgun] men were throwing Arab corpses into a house from the roof, while a huge fire was burning. It was really like a crematorium. Besides that horror, I saw many wood fires along the path on which corpses were burning. The stench in the air was unbearable."[187]

A commander of Haganah later recalled:

"I saw cut-off genitalia and women's crushed stomachs. It was direct murder. Soldiers shot everyone they saw, including women and children. Parents begged commanders to stop the slaughter, to please stop shooting."[188]

Many people reading those accounts will find parallels with what Hamas is claimed to have done to Israelis in October, 2023, and Hamas – indeed all Palestinians – were described as 'human animals' by an Israeli minister, but we'll return to that point later.[189]

At the time, April 1948, this massacre was widely publicised. In fact, the Zionists were not unhappy that the news got out, because it was a useful tool in terrifying Palestinians in other villages that this might be their fate if they didn't leave their homes for the Jews to take over.

Menahem Begin, a leader of the group that committed the atrocity, and later prime minister of Israel, summarized the effect of the slaughter of innocents at Deir Yassin. "Without what was done at Deir Yassin there would not have been a State of Israel," he wrote in his book, *The Revolt*.

The massacre generated a question in the British parliament, with a resigned reply from a minister:

"MR. PETER THORNEYCROFT: If I heard aright, the right hon. Gentleman said that the Irgun had a more or less official Press conference, at which they announced that they had successfully perpetrated this outrage and correspondents, British and American, attended. If this took place, why were not arrests made on the spot?

MR. CREECH JONES: What I said was that a Jewish representative had met American and Jewish correspondents and had conveyed the information to these correspondents of this battle in the hills, but beyond that we have no knowledge." [190]

If Deir Yassin had been unique, a group of rogue terrorists going berserk, say, it would have been bad enough. But in fact, over the years it has become clear that around the same time there were many more similar massacres, unreported and with perpetrators who went unpunished. At the risk of piling Pelion upon Ossa, here are some more accounts of Zionist atrocities against Palestinians, taken from an Israeli newspaper article about details of massacres contained in classified Israel archives.[191]

In the village of Al-Burj (today Modi'in) in July 1948, four elderly men remained in the village after its capture. Three of them were taken to an isolated house and six hand grenades were thrown into the house. They killed an elderly man and two women. Afterward the house was torched, burning the three bodies. When the fourth man returned, he was told that the three others had been sent to the hospital in Ramallah. Apparently he didn't believe the story, and a few hours later he too was put to death, with four bullets.

In the Meron region, members of the Irgun, killed with a machine gun 35 Arabs who had surrendered to that company with a white flag in their hands. They took as captives peaceful residents, among them women and children, ordered them to dig a pit, pushed them into it with long French bayonets and shot them until they were all murdered. These included a woman with an infant in her arms. Arab children of about 13 or 14 who were playing with grenades were all shot. A girl of about 19-20 was raped by men from another Irgun unit. Afterward she was stabbed with a bayonet and a wooden stick was thrust into her body.

The village of Hula was conquered by a company of the Carmeli Brigade, 22nd battalion, under the command of Shmuel Lahis. Hundreds of residents fled but about 60 people remained in the village and surrendered without resistance. Lahis ordered the removal of fifteen Arabs from the house they were in and led them to an isolated building. When they got there, Lahis ordered the Arabs to be taken into one of the rooms and there he made them stand in a line with their faces to the wall. Lahis then shot the Arabs with a Sten gun. After they fell, he checked the bodies. Some of them still showed signs of life and Lahis then fired additional shots into them.

The villages of Saliha, Safsaf and Al-Dawayima lay close to the border with Lebanon. The 7th Brigade executed between 60 and 80 inhabitants by concentrating residents in a building in the village and then blowing up the structure with the people inside.

In Safsaf near Safed, soldiers from the 7th Brigade massacred dozens of inhabitants. According to one testimony, fifty-two men were caught, tied to one another, made to dig a pit and shot. Women came, and begged for mercy. There were 61 bodies, and evidence of three cases of rape."

In the village of Al-Dawayima, troops of the 8th Brigade massacred about a hundred people. A soldier who witnessed the events described to officials what happened: "There was no battle and no resistance. The first conquerors killed 80 to 100 Arab men, women and children. The children were killed by smashing their skulls with sticks. There wasn't a house without people killed in it."[192] An Arab woman with her newborn baby was made to clean the place for a couple of days, and then they shot her and the baby. According to an intelligence officer, the number of those killed was 120.

In the village of Reineh, near Nazareth, 14 Arabs were murdered at the beginning of September, among them a Bedouin woman and also a member of the Land of Israel Workers Alliance, Yusuf al-Turki. They were seized next to the village, accused of smuggling, taken to the village and murdered. The victim's families claimed that those murdered had been carrying hundreds of liras, a very substantial amount.

An anonymous soldier in the journal *Ner* related after the war how his comrades in the IDF unit had murdered an elderly Arab woman who remained behind during the conquest of the village of Lubiya, in Lower Galilee: "This became a fashion. And when I complained to the battalion commander about what was going on, and asked him to put a stop to the rampage, which has no military justification, he shrugged his shoulders and said that 'there is no order from above' to prevent it. Since then the battalion just descended further down the slope and the atrocities multiplied."

For decades, survivors of the many massacres carried out by Israeli terrorists and sometimes by the Israeli regular army have tried to tell their stories but been dismissed as liars. Meron Benvenisti, an Israeli political scientist commented on some of the events described above:

"These atrocities – which fifty years later are regarded as libel, invented by the enemies of Israel, and whose retelling is perceived as an example of the rewriting of history by revisionist historians – were, at the time they took place, known to

134

ministers in the Israeli government, military commanders, and even the general public. The government set up commissions of its own, but the work of these bodies came to naught because soldiers and officers refused to testify against their comrades in arms. Prime Minister Ben-Gurion hid the 'shameful deeds' from the public."[193]

Norman Finkelstein, an American historian writes:

"By 1948, the Jew was not only able to 'defend himself' but to commit massive atrocities as well. Indeed, according to the former director of the Israeli army archives, 'in almost every village occupied by us during the War of Independence, acts were committed which are defined as war crimes, such as murders, massacres, and rapes' ... Uri Milstein, the authoritative Israeli military historian of the 1948 war, goes one step further, maintaining that 'every skirmish ended in a massacre of Arabs.'"[194]

It should not be assumed that every Jew in the new state was complicit in these horrors. In fact, although there are many more such massacres than the ones I mention above, I have concentrated on those because, unusually, documents confirming them have slipped through the heavily classified Israeli archives. These specific events were discussed among Israeli cabinet ministers in November 1948. The minutes of their discussion reveal a certain amount of heart-searching among some at least of the members attending.

SHAPIRA: The situation in this matter is like a plague. Today the committee heard one witness, and I buried my face in my hands, in shame and disgrace. If this is the situation, I don't know from which side a greater danger exists to the state – from the side of the Arabs or from our own side. In my opinion, all our moral foundations have been undermined and we need to look for ways to curb these instincts. We have reached this state of affairs because we did not know how to control things when this first started. My impression is that we are living in a fools' paradise. If no shift occurs, then we are undermining the government's moral basis with our own hands."

AGRICULTURE MINISTER AHARON ZISLING (MAPAM): "I received a letter from a certain person about this matter. ... After reading the letter I received, I couldn't sleep the whole night. I felt that something was being done that was affecting my soul, the soul of my home and the soul of all of us here. I could not imagine where we had come from and where we are going. I know that this is not a chance thing but something that determines the nation's standards of life. I know that this could have consequences in every area of our life. One transgression generates another, and this matter becomes people's second nature."

TRANSPORTATION MINISTER DAVID REMEZ: "We have slid down a terrible slope – true, not the whole army, but if there are deeds like these and they are recurring in quite a few places, they are undoubtedly horrific to the point of despair."

REMEZ: "These deeds remove us from the category of Jews and from the category of human beings altogether. Precisely on these grave matters we have been silent to this day. We must find a way to put a stop to these deeds, but we must not silence our conscience by placing the whole gravity of the blame on boys who were dragged in the wake of deeds that were done earlier."

MINISTER SHAPIRA stated: "The fact is that the soldiers are afraid to testify. I asked one soldier whether he would be willing to appear before the committee. He asked me not to mention his name, to forget that he spoke with me and to consider him someone who doesn't know a thing."

I am intrigued by the remark by David Remez – "These deeds remove us from the category of Jews and from the category of human beings altogether." It is so close to the words the Israeli defence minister, Yoav Gallant, was to utter 75 years later, describing the Palestinian fighters as "human animals."

But the scruples of a few ministers were not enough to change the situation or to achieve some kind of prosecution of the many Jews who had carried out these acts. Ben-Gurion was the prime minister, and he had no interest in a thorough investigation of war crimes, as Adam Raz, the researcher who unearthed the minutes of these meetings, commented:

> "[Ben-Gurion] refused to grant the committee of three the authority to subpoena witnesses, and blamed its members' laziness for its failure. Whereas some ministers demanded the establishment of a committee with teeth and urged that those responsible be brought to justice, Ben-Gurion pulled in a completely opposite direction. The meeting ended with the following decision: 'The government assigns to the prime minister [responsibility for] investigating all of the claims made about the army's behaviour vis-a-vis Arabs in the Galilee and the south.'"

I have resisted drawing parallels which may already be occurring in the minds of readers, but now is the time to do so.

First, any atrocity Israel describes today among the actions of Hamas on October 7th 2023, can be matched with an atrocity carried out by Jews in 1947-8. (In fact, many of the worst accusations by Israel in 2023 have not been supported by evidence, whereas the cabinet ministers meeting in 1948 leaves no doubt that those atrocities *did* happen.)

Second, people who believe that the killing, maiming, and mutilating of Palestinians in Gaza is 'self-defence' need their heads examined. The capacity of Israelis to commit the acts described above did not evaporate in 1948, but has been present in some Israelis ever since. There have even been similar attacks on Palestinians years after Israel gained its independence. The interested reader can research places called Qibya, or Kafr Qasim, or Rishon LeZion, or Sabra and Shatila or Cave of the Patriarchs, for starters.

And I have to point this out: the hatred of Arabs that *must* have been in the hearts of the Jews who massacred and raped in 1948, seems comparable to what we can infer about the hatred of the SS and the Gestapo for their victims as they carried out similar massacres.

There is a pair of uncannily similar events that brings out that parallel starkly.

A: Soldiers arrived in a town and ordered everyone to assemble in the town square. Women and children were then locked in a building while the soldiers looted the village. Nearly 200 men were taken to some nearby barns, which were set on fire. Six men survived. The soldiers then set fire to the building with the women and children and 247 women and 205 children died.

B: Soldiers arrived in a town and started going from house to house, looting and killing the occupants. A number of men, some armed with old rifles, took shelter in a building. The soldiers killed a total of 426 men, women and children, including 176 men sheltering in the building.

One of these is a German attack on a French village, the other a Jewish attack on an Arab village. In one, the building where the men were killed was a mosque, in the other a church.

The Jewish attack on Arabs had an extra element. The entire surviving population of the town, which was in the area allocated to the Arabs in the UN partition plan, was expelled and forced to march east in the July sun. Old men, women and children, 50-70,000 of them many dying of thirst in the July heat, ended up in the West Bank, which Israel was to occupy 19 years later.*

What point am I making here?

I am not saying that all Jews are crypto Nazis, or indeed that any are. But I am saying that there is no justification for Israel's self-righteousness on the world stage. There is *nothing* special about Israel, or Jews, or Judaism, as claimed in the fake history of how Israel came to be, both in its Biblical 'history' which most unprejudiced historians see as myth rather than truth, and in its tendentious accounts of the events from 1917 to 1948, of which the 'five armies' fabrication is just one element. Israel is a nation like any other, with good and bad people, sinners and saints, liars and honest men. And believe it or not, so is Palestine.

---

* The town in the A was Oradour, in the middle of France; in B, there were two adjacent towns, Lydda and Ramleh, which after being emptied were taken over and eventually included in Israel.

138

If Israel's actions in the 2023-4 Gaza war have achieved anything positive, it is that many people, particularly young people, no longer believe what Israel's leaders are trying to tell them, and have begun to realise that there is an alternative history to that propagated by Israel and its supporters.

Rashid Khalidi, a leading Palestinian academic, in an interview in 2024:

> "I grew up in a world where there was no Palestinian voice in the Arab world, in the public sphere in the West; none at all, it didn't exist. Palestinians didn't exist. My four grandchildren are growing up in a time when there are quite vigorous voices for Palestine, all over the world. So that's an element of change for the better. I grew up in a world in which the Zionist narrative was completely hegemonic and Israel was fulsomely described as 'a light unto the nations'. That is no longer the case. Today it is widely, and rightly, seen as a pariah state because of its own genocidal actions. These are among the few good things that have happened in these very bad times."[195]

Until Israel rejects Yitzhak Shamir's principal that 'it is permissible to lie to benefit Israel'; until it eliminates racism from its official discourse; until it accepts that true democracy recognises the full rights of Palestinians in Israel as well as the rights of Palestinians elsewhere to a state of their own; until it stops using the Holocaust as a shield for its own misdeeds; and until it forswears the kind of officially-sanctioned violence that kills innocent men, woman and children, Israel will deserve to be treated as that pariah state.

And one final point:

As I write this at the end of 2024, I look at Israel and its ordinary citizens and I wonder, is it all worth it for them? What is it that terrifies them about the mere possibility of a Palestine state? Do they prefer the regular bouts of attack and defence, retaliation and 'pretaliation'? Do ordinary Israelis like being blamed around the world for the war crimes and genocide carried out in their name, and the regular recourses to bomb shelters and total evacuation of large areas of the country? Is this really better than allowing a Palestinian state to exist on the West Bank and in Gaza, areas which, in any case, were not part of the original area allocated to the Jews in the UN Partition Plan? Or even, as I described in another book[1], is the current situation really better than sharing a single state with Palestinians between the Jordan and the Mediterranean?

On my last trip to Palestine, I was driven from an event at lunchtime in Ramallah in the Occupied West Bank to dinner with a friend in Jaffa in Israel. It was during a period of relative calm, and we passed easily through checkpoints from one territory to the other. Looking at the customers in both restaurants, I would not have the faintest idea who was an Arab and who a Jew. The range of facial types among each ethnic group made it impossible to identify anyone as unambiguously a Jew or an Arab if they were not wearing characteristic headwear. There was no obvious transition between the two territories on my journey, other than the point at which we drove without stopping through a checkpoint at the notorious Wall, and not much difference in the experiences at either end. The buildings seen on the way were similar – neat, regimented Jewish housing alternating with more traditional stone Arab villages, in both territories; good quality highways with worse minor roads, in both territories; buses plying their routes, similar-looking soldiers and police, in different uniforms; mobile phone reception, and so on. There were even pockets of poverty in both territories – refugee camps in one; Oriental Jews herded into poor housing in the other.

I am not trying to say that the two communities could be welded seamlessly into one, if the whole area became a single state. Nevertheless, for me that trip presented a vision of what a single state might be like. On the ground, it seems eminently possible. Comparing it with German reunification, paradoxically it is Israel's increasing grip on Palestinian areas that would make such a change easier. Roads, water systems, communications, the media, all share systems in a way which

---

[1] *A Modest Proposal*, Karl Sabbagh, Skyscraper Publications, 2018

the two Germanys never did. I made a television documentary about the problems of reuniting the two halves of Berlin after 1989, and from railways which changed gauge at the border to incompatible telephones and sewage systems, the problems were far greater than the technical problems of reuniting the Occupied Territories and Israel.

Apart from frank racism, which as we've seen was in the minds of many Zionists during the first half of the 20th century, what would the average Israeli find objectionable about seeing the occasional Arab in her street or in the supermarket or on the beach? Or even about sharing ideas on the governance of Israel/Palestine between Arab and Jewish parliamentarians? Or about eating in an Arab restaurant side by side with Arab families? (Israel has already hijacked hummus and falafel in their own restaurants.)

Would the hardships of sharing the land with Palestinians really be worse than keeping on the alert for sirens, dashing into shelters, dying in terrorist attacks, and feeling the weight of opprobrium from ordinary people round the world who currently see Israel as a pariah state.

I'm just asking.

Principal books quoted

Ben-Gurion: The Burning Ground 1886-1948, Shabtai Teveth, Lume Books, 1988

Expulsion of the Palestinians, Nur Masalha, Institute of Palestinian Studies, 1992

In the Shadow of the Holocaust, Yosef Grodzinsky, Common Courage Press, 2004

Middle East Diary 1917-1956, Richard Meinertzhagen, Thomas Yoseloff, 1959

Nisi Dominus, Nevill Barbour, George G. Harrap, London, 1946

One Palestine Complete, Tom Segev, Picador, 2001

Palestine: Land of Broken Promises, O.S. Edwardes, Dorothy Crisp & Co, 1946

Palestine Papers, Doreen Ingrams, John Murray, 1972

Palestine Reborn, Walid Khalidi, I.B. Tauris, 1992

Palestine: The Reality, J.M.N. Jeffries, Longman, 1939

Promise and Fulfilment: Palestine 1917-1949, Arthur Koestler, 1949

Righteous Victims, Benny Morris, Vintage, 2001

State of Terror, Thomas Suarez, Skyscraper Publications, 2017

The Birth of Israel, Jorge Garcia-Granados, Alfred A. Knopf, 1949

The Birth of Israel, Simha Flapan, Pantheon, 1988

The Ethnic Cleansing of Palestine, Ilan Pappé, Oneworld, 2007

The Jewish National Home, 1917-1942, Paul Goodman, Zionist Federation of Great Britain and Ireland, J.M. Dent, 1943

The Gentile Zionists, N.A.Rose, Frank Cass, London 1973

The Palestine Diary, Robert John, Samuel Hadawi, 2 vols, 1970

The Rise of Israel, Vols 1-39, Garland Publishing, Inc. New York, 1987

The War for Palestine, Eugene L. Rogan, Avi Shlaim, (eds), Cambridge, 2001

Quotations in this book from UK Parliamentary Debates can be found on the Hansard Archive site, at the appropriate date given in the text: https://api.parliament.uk/historic-hansard/index.html

Index

144

145

146

Endnotes

[1] Quoted in *Righteous Victims,* Benny Morris, Vintage, 2001, p. 140

[2] *Hansard*, 26 January, 1948

[3] https://www.bbc.co.uk/news/world-middle-east-54116567

[4] *The Arab Refugee Problem,* Joseph B. Schectman, Philosophical Library, New York (1952), pp. 5–6

[5] https://archive.nytimes.com/learning.blogs.nytimes.com/2011/11/29/nov-29-1947-united-nations-partitions-palestine-allowing-for-creation-of-israel/

[6] https://www.972mag.com/why-did-israeli-historians-whitewash-a-short-artillery-attack/

[7] https://www.gov.il/BlobFolder/generalpage/facts-about-israel-2018/en/English _ABOUT_ISRAEL_PDF_Quest-for-Peace.pdf

[8] https://www.jstor.org/stable/23535809

[9] https://www.archives.gov/milestone-documents/press-release-announcing-us-recognition-of-israel

[10] *, Zionism*: *The Saga of a National Liberation Movement,* Jacob Tsur, 1977,p. 88,

[11] https://www.factsandlogic.org/hotline/2003 [FLAME]

[12] https://www.jewishhistory.org/the-miracle-of-israel/

[13] *Hansard*, 26 January, 1949

[14] *Zionism and the Jewish Future*, Ed. H. Sacher, p.10

[15] Moshe Smilansky, quoted in *Righteous Victims: A History of the Zionist-Arab Conflict, 1881-2001*, Benny Morris, Random House, 2001, p. 43

[16] *Expulsion of the Palestinians*, Nur Masalha, Institute of Palestinian Studies, 1992, p. 6

[17] *The Jewish National Home, 1917-1942,* Paul Goodman, Zionist Federation of Great Britain and Ireland, J.M. Dent, 1943, p. 227

[18] *Expulsion of the Palestinians*, Nur Masalha, Institute of Palestinian Studies, p. 17

[19] Ibid p. 29

[20] *One Palestine Complete*, Tom Segev, Picador, 2001, p. 104

[21] *The Innocents Abroad*, Mark Twain, p. 485

[22] Ibid, p. 481, 520, 546

[23] *Promised Land,* E. Thorbecke, Harper and Brothers 1947, p. 102

[24] *The Letters and Papers of Chaim Weizmann*, Series A, Letters, Volume VII, Israel Universities Press, Jerusalem, 1975, p. 86-7

[25] *The Rise of Israel,* Vol. 8, Isaiah Friedman (ed.), Garland Publishing, Inc. New York, 1987, p. 28

[26] Ibid, p. 26

[27] Ibid, p. 36

[28] *The Rise of Israel,* Vol. 8, Isaiah Friedman (ed), Garland, 1987, p. 39

[29] *Philosophy Now, The Paradoxes of Arthur Balfour*, Tim Madigan, https://philosophynow.org/issues/81/The_Paradoxes_of_Arthur_Balfour

[30] President Wilson's Message to Congress, January 8, 1918; Records of the United States Senate; Record Group 46.

[31] Statement by the British government for the Peace Conference concerning the settlement of the Middle East, Henry Churchill King Papers, 1873-1934, RG 2/6, box 128, folder 2

[32] https://digitallibrary.un.org/record/829707?v=pdf

[33] Hexter to Warburg, August 23, 1931, File 3, Box 2, MBH, quoted in *The American Jewish Archives Journal*, Volume LIV Number 1 (2002), p. 33

[34], *A Jewish Palestine: The Jewish Case for a British Trusteeship,* H. Sacher, Zionist Organisation, London 1919, p. 17, quoted in Tom Segev, *One Palestine Complete*, p. 119

[35] *The Rape of Palestine: A Mandate Chronology*, Blake Alcott, https://blakealcott.jimdofree.com/publications/

[36] Tenth Zionist Congress, Basle, 1911, speech by the President, quoted by Nevill Barbour, *Nisi Dominus*, George G. Harrap, London, 1946, p. 51

[37] Memorandum by Kinahan Cornwallis, Director of the Arab Bureau in Cairo, on the (Zionist) Commission on the 20th April, 1918, quoted in *Palestine Papers*, Doreen Ingrams, John Murray, 1972 p. 28

[38] Quoted, *Palestine:The Reality*, in J. M. N. Jeffries, Longmans, Green and Co, 1939, p. 267

[39] Churchill White Paper, 1922, https://avalon.law.yale.edu/ 20th_century/brwh1922.asp

[40] *Nisi Dominus*, Nevill Barbour, George G. Harrap, London, 1946, p. 66

[41] *Palestine Papers*, Doreen Ingrams, John Murray, 1972, p. 13-14

[42] Quoted in Aaron S. Klieman, editor, *The Rise of Israel*, Vol. 17, Garland Publishing, 1987, pp. 163

[43] Col. Stewart F. Newcombe, note accompanying letter to *Times*, May 30th 1939, in MEC, Barbour Box II, File 3

[44] *Nisi Dominus*, Nevill Barbour, George G. Harrap, London, 1946, p. 66

[45] Quoted in *The Israel-Arab Reader*, edited by Walter Laqueur, Penguin Books, London, 1970, pp. 47-9

[46] *The Birth of Israel*, Simha Flapan, pp 23-4l

[47] *The Palestine Diary*, Robert John, Samuel Hadawi, Vol 2, p. 1

[48] Motion adopted at Labour Party Conference, quoted by Frederick Cocks M.P. in *Hansard*, 9 Dec 1948

[49] *Middle East Diary 1917-1956*, Richard Meinertzhagen, Thomas Yoseloff, 1959, p. 52

[50] Ibid, p. 58

[51] Ibid, p. 66

[52] *Palestine Papers*, Doreen Ingrams, John Murray, 1972, p. 58

[53] *Palestine Papers*, Doreen Ingrams, John Murray, 1972, p.146

[54] Ibid, p. 149

[55] Ibid, p. 151-2

[56] *Palestine Papers*, Doreen Ingrams, John Murray, 1972, p. 155

[57] *The Rise of Israel*, Isaiah Friedman (ed), Vol 25, Garland, p. 322

[58] *Palestine: The Reality*, J.M.N. Jeffries, Longman, 1939, pp. 454-5

[59] Sir W. Joynson-Hicks, M.P. House of Commons debate, 4th July, 1922

[60] Winston Churchill M.P. House of Commons debate, 4th July, 1922
[61] Sir W. Joynson-Hicks, M.P. *Hansard*, House of Commons debate, 4th July, 1922
[62] Sir J. Butcher, *Hansard*, House of Commons debate, 4th July, 1922

[63] Ibid, 457-8

[64] *Promise and Fulfilment: Palestine 1917-1949*, Arthur Koestler, 1949, Pp 34-35.

[65] Ibid, pp 199-200.

[66] *Nisi Dominus*, Nevill Barbour, George G. Harrap, London, 1946 p. 135

[67] *Problems de la renaissance juive*, Y. Buchmil (Jerusalem, 1936), p. 284

[68] *No Ease in Zion*, Tosco Fyvel, A. A. Knopf, p. 176

[69] David Hacohen, Mapai leader quoted in *Expulsion of the Palestinians*, Nur Masalha, Institute for Palestine Studies, 1992 p. 25

[70] Presentation of Haim Kalvaryski entitled: *Relation with the Arab Neighbors*, Central Zionist Archive (CZA) J1/8777.

[71] *Palestine: Correspondence with the Palestine Arab Delegation and the Zionist Organisation*, June, 1922. His Majesty's Stationery Office. Cmd. 1700

[72] *Palestine: The Reality*, J.M.N. Jeffries, Longman, 1939, p. 685

[73] *World Affairs*, Philip Hitti, March, 1946, Vol. 109, No. 1 (March, 1946), pp. 7-9
[74] *The Gentile Zionists,* N.A.Rose, Frank Cass, London 1973, p. 14

[75] *The Rise of Israel*, Isaiah Friedman (ed), Vol 18, Garland, p 179
[76] *The Rise of Israel* Aaron S. Klieman (ed), Vol 20, Garland, p.267

[77] Namier, quoted in N.A.Rose, *The Gentile Zionists*, Frank Cass, London 1973. p. 22

[78] *Jewish National Home*, Ephraim Broido, p. 227,

[79] *Middle East Diary 1917-1956*, Richard Meinertzhagen, Thomas Yoseloff, 1959, p. 103

[80] *Palestine: The Reality*, J.M.N. Jeffries, Longman, 1939 p. 685

[81] *The Gentile Zionists,* N.A.Rose, Frank Cass, London 1973, p. 41

[82] Ibid, p. 42

[83] Evidence Submitted to Palestine Royal Commission by M.V. Jabotinsky, p 28

[84] Quoted in *Nisi Dominus*, Nevill Barbour, George G. Harrap, London, 1946, p. 162

[85] Quoted in *Palestine: Land of Broken Promises*, O.S. Edwardes, Dorothy Crisp & Co, 1946, p. 38

[86] Ibid

[87] *Palestine: Land of Broken Promises*, O.S. Edwardes, Dorothy Crisp & Co, 1946, p. 35-6

[88] *Nisi Dominus*, Nevill Barbour, George G. Harrap, London, 1946, p. 175

[89] *The Rise of Israel*, Isaiah Friedman (ed), Vol 25, Garland p. 367-8

[90] Ibid, p. 330

[91] *The Gentile Zionists,* N.A.Rose, Frank Cass, London 1973, p. 140

[92] *Hansard* quoted in *The Rise of Israel*, Isaiah Friedman (ed), Vol 25, Garland p. 45

[93] *Statement of Policy*, July 7th, 1937, H.M. Stationery Office, Cmd 6019

[94] *Nisi Dominus*, Nevill Barbour, George G. Harrap, London, 1946, p. 179

[95] *Statement of Policy*, July 7th, 1937, H.M. Stationery Office, Cmd 6019

[96] *Palestine Through the Fog of Propaganda*, M. E. Abcarius, Hutchinson, 1946, p. 219

[97] Quoted in *One Palestine Complete*, Tom Segev 1999, p 465 note 64

[98] *The Birth of the Palestinian Refugee Problem Revisited*, Benny Morris, CUP, 2004, p. 59

[99] www.sullivan-county.com/x/1921.htm

[100] *In the Shadow of the Holocaust*, Yosef Grodzinsky, Common Courage Press, 2004, p. 59

[101] Ibid, p. 41

[102] *Ben-Gurion: The Burning Ground 1886-1948*, Shabtai Teveth, Lume Books, pp 855-56.

[103] *In the Shadow of the Holocaust*, Yosef Grodzinsky, Common Courage Press, 2004, p. 50

[104] *In the Shadow of the Holocaust*, Yosef Grodzinsky, Common Courage Press, 2004, p. 94

[105] *The Birth of Israel,* Jorge Garcia-Granados, Alfred A. Knopf, 1949, p. 218

[106] *In the Shadow of the Holocaust*, Yosef Grodzinsky, Common Courage Press, 2004, p. 97

[107] Ibid p. 97

[108] Ibid p. 99

[109] Quoted from *Brif zu Abrashn (Letters to Abrash)* Chava Rosenfarb, Tel Aviv: Y.L. Peretz Publishers, 1992 pp 800-801

[110] *The Birth of Israel*, Jorge Garcia-Granados, Alfred A. Knopf, 1949, pp 227-8

[111] UN General Assembly, held at Lake Success, New York, on Friday, 10 October 1947, www.documents.un.org

[112] *In the Shadow of the Holocaust*, Yosef Grodzinsky, Common Courage Press, 2004, p. 48

[113] *In the Shadow of the Holocaust*, Yosef Grodzinsky, Common Courage Press, 2004, p.188

[114] Ibid p.191

[115] Ibid p.191

[116] Ibid p 227

[117] *Unser tsait*, June 1948, p33

[118] *In the Shadow of the Holocaust*, Yosef Grodzinsky, Common Courage Press, 2004, p. 192

[119] Ibid p. 199

[120] Ibid p. 201

[121] Ibid p. 201

[122] *New York Times*, January 10th, 1999

[123] Speech at Hebrew University, Jerusalem, by Judah Magnes, Chancellor, 1929

[124] *New York Times*, July 18, 1937

[125] Speech by Judah Magnes, 18 August 1937, *Jud. Press Zentrale*, Zurich, No, 956

[126] *The Birth of the Palestinian Refugee Problem Revisited*, Benny Morris Cambridge University Press, 2004, p. 52-3

[127] *Hansard, House iof Commons*, 25 February 1947 vol 433

[128] *Mandate Days*, A.J. Sherman, Thames and Hudson, 1997, p. 178

[129] Quoted in *Anti Zionism*, ed. by Teikener, Abed-Rabbo & Mezvinsky, 1988

[130] Harry S. Truman diary, Monday July 21, 1947   https://www.trumanlibrary.gov/library/research-files/harry-s-truman-diary-entry?documentid=NA&pagenumber=3

[131] *Hansard*, House of Commons, 18 February 1947 vol 433 cc 985-94

[132] *The Palestine Diary,* Robert John, Samuel Hadawi, *Vol* 2, pp.117-8

[133] *The Birth of Israel*, Jorge Garcia-Granados, Alfred A. Knopf, 1949, p. 4

[134] Ibid p. 25

[135] Ibid, p. 32

[136] Ibid p. 68

[137] Ibid, p. 27

[138] Ibid p. 59

[139] Ibid, p. 67

[140] Ibid, p. 244-6

[141] Ibid p. 244-6

[142] Tenth meeting, UN, held at Lake Success, New York, on Friday, 10 October 1947, documents.un.org

[143] Ibid

[144] Ibid

[145] *Palestine Reborn*, Walid Khalidi, I.B. Tauris, 1992, p. 59

[146] Ibid

[147] CIA reports on Palestine: https://www.jewishvirtuallibrary.org/cia-daily-summaries-regarding-partition-and-the-1948-war?utm_content=cmp-true

[148] *The Palestine Diary,* Robert John, Samuel Hadawi, Vol, p.265-66

[149] Ibid

[150] *The Rise of Israel*, Isaiah Friedman (ed), Vol 37, Garland, p. 196

[151] *Israel in the Mind of America,* Peter Grose, Alfred A. Knopf, 1983, p. 248

[152] *The Palestine Diary*, Robert John, Samuel Hadawi, Vol 2, p. 262

[153] Memorandum by Harold Beeley, 9 January 1948, F.O. 371/68528

[154] *Middle East Diary 1917-1956*, Richard Meinertzhagen, Thomas Yoseloff, 1959 Entry for August 10th

[155] *Palestine Reborn*, Walid Khalidi, I.B. Tauris & Co, p. 63

[156] *The Rise of Israel*, Isaiah Friedman (ed), Vol 37, Garland, p. 150

[157] *Memoirs of Harry S. Truman*, Smithmark, 1955, p. 158

[158] *Jerusalem Post*, Abraham Rabinovich, March 8th, 2002, quoted in http://www.palestineremembered.com/Acre/PalestineRemembered/Story780.html

[159] *The Fateful Triangle*, Noam Chomsky, quoted in *The Origin of The Palestine-Israel Conflict, Third Edition* (Including Intifada 2000) Published By Jews For Justice In The Middle East, http://www.cactus48.com/truth.html

[160] *The Rise of Israel*, Isaiah Friedman (ed), Vol 25, Garland, p 331

[161] *The Ethnic Cleansing of Palestine,* Ilan Pappé, Oneworld, p. 28

[162] *Palestine Reborn*, Walid Khalidi, I.B. Tauris & Co, p. 73

[163] *State of Terror,* Thomas Suarez, Skyscraper Publications, 2017 p. 228

[164] Ibid

[165] Ibid, p. 229

[166] These accounts taken from *The Palestine Diary*, Robert John, Samuel Hadawi, vol. 2, pp 288-93

[167] *Palestine Reborn*, Walid Khalidi, I.B. Tauris & Co, p. 74

[168] Ibid, p. 75

[169] *Selected Documents on the 1948 Palestine War*, Walid Khalidi, *Journal of Palestine Studies,* Spring, 1998, Vol. 27, No. 3, p. 100

[170] *The Rise of Israel*, Isaiah Friedman (ed), Vol 30, Garland 30, p. 59

[171] *Palestine, The Arabs and Israel,* Henry Cattan quoted in *The Origin Of The Palestine-Israel Conflict*, Third Edition (Including Intifada 2000) Published By Jews For Justice In The Middle East, http://www.cactus48.com/truth.html

[172] CIA reports on Palestine: https://www.jewishvirtuallibrary.org/cia-daily-summaries-regarding-partition-and-the-1948-war?utm_content=cmp-true

[173] *Journal of Palestine Studies*, Spring, 1998, Vol. 27, No. 3, Walid Khalidi, pp. 60

[174] *The Iron Wall,* Avi Shlaim, W.W. Norton, 2000, p. 34

[175] *The War for Palestine*, Eugene L. Rogan, Avi Shlaim, (eds), Rashid Khalidi, p. 30

[176] *The Rise of Israel*, Isaiah Friedman (ed), Vol 39, Garland, p. 155

[177] Rashid Khalidi, personal communication

[178] 'Siha Im Abdallah, 17.11.47' ('Conversation with Abdallah, 17 November 1947'), Ezra Danin, Central Zionist Archives, S25/4004.

[179] *The Collusion That Never Was: King Abdallah, the Jewish Agency and the Partition of Palestine*, Efraim Karsh, *Journal of Contemporary History*, Vol. 34, No. 4 (Oct., 1999), pp. 569-585

[180] *The Palestine Diary*, Robert John, Samuel Hadawi, Vol 2, p. 295

[181] Quoted in *The War for Palestine*, Eugene L. Rogan, Avi Shlaim, (eds), Cambridge, 2001, p. 84

[182] *The Rise of Israel*, Isaiah Friedman (ed), Vol 39, Garland, p. 28

[183] It is interesting that the UK dismissed the 2017 UN General Assembly vote about Britain's refusal to hand back the Chagos islands because it was 'non-binding.' What a shame it didn't dismiss, on similar grounds, the General Assembly vote to partition Palestine.

[184] *The Birth of Israel,* Simha Flapan, Pantheon, 1988, p. 198-199

[185] *New Star in the Near East*, Kenneth W. Bilby, Doubleday, 1950, p. 33

[186] https://mondoweiss.net/2024/04/the-deir-yassin-massacre-reminds-us-every-zionist-accusation-is-a-confession/

[187] Ibid

[188] Ibid

[189] See https://mondoweiss.net/2024/04/the-deir-yassin-massacre-reminds-us-every-zionist-accusation-is-a-confession/

[190] *Hansard*, 12th April 1948

[191] *Haaretz*, Adam Raz, Dec 9 2021

[192] Testimony of an Israeli soldier who participated in the massacre at al Duwayima Village, on 29th October 1948. Quoted in *Davar*, 9th. June 1979

[193] Meron Benvenisti, *Sacred Landscape:* The Buried History of the Holy Land since 1948, University of California Press, 2000, Berkeley, pp. 152-153

[194], *Image and Reality of the Israel-Palestine Conflict*, Norman Finkelstein quoted in *The Origin Of The Palestine-Israel Conflict* (Third Edition) (Including Intifada 2000) Published By Jews For Justice In The Middle East, http://www.cactus48.com/truth.html

[195] *New Left Review*, May/June, 2024 p. 38

Printed in Great Britain
by Amazon